CW00409692

Contents

The Bunch of Grapes, on the corner of Silver Street and Whiteheads Lane. Beyond it, until 1958, stood the New Bear Inn (the Old Bear, now plain The Bear, was opposite). The New Bear and The Swan were the town's two foremost Inns.

Bradford on Avon's Pubs and Breweries

~

Jack Mock

Cheers!

EX LIBRIS PRESS

Published in 2012 by
Ex Libris Press
11 Regents Place
Bradford on Avon
Wiltshire   BA15 1ED

Origination by Ex Libris Press
Typseset in 9/12 point Palatino

Printed by Anthony Rowe
Chippenham   Wiltshire

ISBN 978-1-906641-40-5

Preface

My first experience of a public house was at the tender age of 18 months. My mother and father, on a summer's evening walk, pushing me in my pram, decided to pop into the Three Horse Shoes for a drink, my father buying his usual pint of beer and my mother a small sherry. They sat outside at a table, with me in the pram alongside. Both drinks were placed on the table. While they were distracted in talking to other customers, I grabbed mother's sherry glass and drank the lot! Their attention was drawn to me when they heard my coughs and splutters. However I survived and slept well that night.

Following early retirement, I was offered a two-year contract which involved full-time research at the Wiltshire Record Office, which was then in Trowbridge. By sheer accident I came across a document that gave information on several Inns, Taverns and Breweries in Bradford, which no longer existed. This was in 1982/3, and it was then that my interest in the subject began. Much earlier I had spent many hours listening to my grandfather Ted and father Bert, two old Bradfordians, reminiscing. In later years to Jack Stafford and Bertram Niblett, both builders and carpenters for many years, who had an extensive knowledge of the buildings and structures of the town. All this helped to sow the seeds of my interest in the pubs of good old Snuffy.

Illness prevented me from completing the project in the 1980s. It was Roger Jones who recently rekindled my enthusiasm to update my research. Thanks to his expertise my project will now be published.

Jack Mock
Bradford on Avon
March 2012

Top: The Brewer; Below: The Cooper (barrel-maker)

Wood engravings by Thomas Bewick, late 18th-early 19th centuries

The Story of Ale

For centuries the townsfolk of Bradford on Avon brewed and drank ale in the town's many ale houses. Indeed, there were reports of so many ale houses in the country, with drunkenness so rife, that between AD 960 and 975 Edgar the Peaceable, King of Wessex, decreed that a large number be closed, with villages permitted the indulgence of only one ale house each. No records exist to show what happened in Bradford.

By the late 12th century the authorities had become more shrewd in their declarations concerning national drinking habits and, in an effort to raise money for the Crusades, Henry II in 1188 introduced the first national tax on ale, called the 'Saladin Tithe'. This was the first instance of such a practice and since then ale and beer have always been taxed in some way.

A more organized form of regulation for the sale of ale and its inspection gradually evolved into the Assize of Bread and Ale Act, 1267. It must be remembered that these were very nearly the two staple items of diet for most people at that time.

As a result local Inspection Officers were annually appointed and sworn in at the Court-Leet for the assize of ale and ale-measures. These officers, called in different localities 'Ale-Founders', 'Ale-Conners' and 'Ale-Tasters' were sworn to examine ale and to take care that the liquor was good and wholesome and that it was sold at the proper assize prices of two gallons for one penny in town and three gallons for one penny out of town. They were also sworn to present dishonest ale vendors to the Court Leet.

Little evidence exists of the Ale-Conner in Bradford, other than a mention by Canon Jones in his *History of Bradford* of 1859. Writing about the town's market he notes:

'The Coroners of the Market had to see generally, that provisions exposed for sale were good in quality and sufficient in quality; that the weights and measures were up to the standard; and, in case of the bread or meat being unfit for food, they had power to order it to be thrown away, and to inflict a fine on the offending bakers or butchers. The using false weights or measures incurred a forfeiture of double the quality of grain or thing sold, and in some instances led to imprisonment. Formerly, there was a separate officer called the Ale-Conner who had to look to the goodness and assize of ale and beer. For very many years no such special officer has been appointed, those just described exercising the general supervision of all things vendible by weight or measure.'

In 1393 King Richard II made it compulsory to display a wooden 'ale-stake' outside each alehouse. The end of each stake would show a bundle of leaves, so that his tasters could clearly identify houses selling ales and ensure that ale brewing was up to the correct standard. The 'ale-stake' was the forerunner to the modern day pub sign – where hops, barley and even grapes are often clearly illustrated.

During the 14th century it was necessary for the ale-tasters to carry out the inspection process regularly, as early wheat-brewed ales did not keep for very long. However, by 1440 barley malt was in common use in the English ale-making process and this was better for the keeping than wheat.

By the end of the 15th century the number of ale-tasters had greatly increased. It is thought that they wore 'Leathern' breeches and, for one of their tests, they sat unmoving for half an hour in a quantity of ale poured into the top of a cask. If their breeches stuck to the wood when they got up, they condemned the beer, because the malt sugar content showed that it had not been properly fermented and was deficient in alcohol.

The use of hops in the liquor-making process was introduced to England from Flanders around 1534. What we now call beer, is actually ale that has some of the dried flowers of the hop plant boiled in it. As hops gradually came into general use, the word 'ale' was retained whether the liquid was hopped or not. Beer brewed with hops kept better and could be stored for longer periods. It is therefore interesting to note that records tell us that Henry VIII, who reigned from 1509 to 1547, would drink only hop-less ale, and Tudor brewers were taken to task for 'ruining' the traditional drink.

An important part of brewing ale is the production of the malt. Traditionally, the maltster in his malthouse germinates the barley grain by wetting it and keeping it warm for about ten days until it shoots. The grain is then dried in a kiln to inhibit further growth and stored until required by the brewer. The brewer then adds the malted and dried grain to water and is boiled. Eventually, after other ingredients are added, the fermentation process is completed and the beer or ale is ready for consumption.

In the early days the brewer often took three fermentations from the must – the pulp of the basic ingredients from which the ale is made. The first was a 'strong' brew, the second a 'middle' strength ale and the third and weakest was a drink called 'small beer' (hence the phrase small beer, meaning of no consequence) which was often given to children as it was only slightly alcoholic.

Many of the water sources in Bradford were impure and sometimes even contaminated through inadequate or non-existent sewers. As the mixtures have to be boiled, this at least purified the water. Often the ale would be unflavoured and taste only of malt. Sometimes herbs, such as yarrow, burdock and even nettle would be boiled with the grain.

Licensing Laws

The licensing laws date from 1552. They were the brainchild of Edward VI, then aged only 15. Young though he was the King was a pious Protestant who abhorred drunkenness – he was, remember, the son of HENRY VIII – and decreed that all Inns in England must henceforth have a licence from the local Justices of the Peace.

Hundreds of alehouses were immediately closed, because Justices of the Peace were told there was now a limit on the number to be allowed in any village or town.

But the new laws said nothing about hours. If innkeepers wanted to remain open round the clock, as before, they could continue to do so. It was a long time before opening hours restrictions were imposed.

In 1599, 1604 and again in 1608, JPs were urged to be extra careful as to how many licences they issued and to whom. In 1618 a Royal Proclamation, endorsed all that the JPs had done and the Assize Judges as they moved around their circuits were to act as general overseers. All went according to plan until the Civil War in 1642 when all orders and decrees from the Privy Council ceased. Therefore by 1688 and the time of the Glorious Revolution, the law had slipped back to a position where very little authority was exercised and licences were issued to all comers.

In 1729 licensees had to apply for a licence each year at the 'Brewster Sessions' of a local Magistrates Court. (In 1989 it was changed to every three years).

By the 1780s, when the Industrial Revolution had already moved large sections of the population from the countryside into the burgeoning towns to take up factory work, alehouse licences were commonly granted on the basis that they must close their doors at a stated hour. This was usually 9pm in winter and 10pm in summer. JPs were responding to the changed times. Factory workers who drank themselves senseless every night impoverished their families and – just as important – were unfit for work

Wilts, to Wit.

IN pursuance of a Precept under the Hands of the REV. J. H. BRADNEY, and EZ. EDMONDS, ESQ., two of HER MAJESTY'S JUSTICES, present at a Petty Sessions, held on the 25th day of July, 1860, at the TOWN HALL, in Bradford, in pursuance of the Statute in that case made and provided, you are to take

NOTICE

THAT A GENERAL

Annual Licencing Meeting,

And SPECIAL SESSIONS of the Justices of the Peace acting for the Division of Bradford, will be held at the TOWN HALL, in Bradford aforesaid, on Wednesday the 29th day of August next, at the hour of Eleven in the Forenoon, of the same day, for the purpose of GRANTING

LICENCES

To persons Keeping, or being about to Keep Inns, Alehouses, and Victualling-Houses, to sell Exciseable Liquors by retail, to be drunk or consumed on the Premises, in such Licences to be specified pursuant to the statute in such case made and provided.

Dated the 27th day of July, 1860.

WILLIAM KENDALL, } High
FRANCIS TAYLOR, } Constables.

J. RAWLING, PRINTER, BRADFORD-ON-AVON.

10

the day after.

These were certainly the motivating forces behind the many Licensing Acts that further restricted the sale of alcohol for the following century right up to 1915.

The setting up in that year of the wartime Liquor Control Board represented the toughest line ever taken by a government on drinking. The Board had unlimited powers and used them to stop all pubs opening before midday, to close early in the afternoon and reopen only between the after-work hour of 5 or 6 in the evening, until 11pm.

The reason for these stringent new hours was indeed the war effort. The Government was anxious workers should be fit for work and also concerned that servicemen at home on leave should not spend all their hours and pay trying to drown their memories of the Front.

Contrary to the above, Bradford magistrates, in common with other West Wiltshire towns, decided to close all pubs at 9 p.m. This was an unpopular decision with many of the town's population.

On 5th February 1915, Police Superintendent Cripps attended the Bradford Licensing Sessions and read his annual report:

'There are 31 ale-houses, 5 "on" beerhouses, 5 "off" beerhouses, 2 grocery licenses and 2 wines and spirits retailers licences, making a total of 45 in the Bradford division.

According to the 1911 census the population of the division was 9,814, this gives an average of 218 persons to each licensed house.

Two persons were convicted this year of drunkenness as against 2 in 1911, 11 in 1912 and 8 in 1913. One licence holder was proceeded against for selling beer in an unsealed vessel to a child. All licences were renewed.'

Less than a month later, in March 1915, Lloyd George made his famous and perhaps contentious claim that the country was fighting 'Germany, Austria and drink; and as far as I can see, the greatest of these three deadly foes is drink.'

The action taken by the Control Board appears to have worked, for after the war they reported to the Government that convictions for drunkenness had numbered 184,000 in 1914 but, by 1918 had fallen to 29,000.

The Control Board was disbanded in 1921 and licensing authority was returned to the magistrates. It is no surprise that JPs clung to the restricted hours. They were convinced the benefits of the new regime could be extended into peacetime, and perhaps indefinitely.

At the Bradford on Avon Petty Sessions at the Town Hall on 1st February 1928, Superintendent Underwood reported there were 45 licensed houses serving a population of 10,112, and that three persons were proceeded against for drunkenness.

During 1939-45, lack of raw materials led to beer shortages and some temporary closure of pubs. However despite these handicaps, they were never busier, certainly in Bradford.

Brewers' troubles persisted in the immediate postwar years, with high levels of taxation, and raw materials were still in short supply. Beer consumption, having risen during the war, resumed the clear downward trend of the pre war period.

By 1960, drunkenness in Bradford was reduced by a half. Bradford's Licensing Magistrates were told that only one person was proceeded against as compared to two the previous year. Police Inspector C. Vincent continued: 'The case of drunkenness was someone of no fixed abode, who was fined 4 shillings (20p). The Police have made regular visits to the licensed houses and these have been conducted satisfactorily.' The Council chairman said, 'I think the licensees are to be congratulated.'

All day Sunday opening for pubs was given the go-ahead from Sunday 6th August 1995. Pubs were allowed to open from 12 noon until 10.30pm. The Act gave licensing committees the power to reimpose all or part of the old Sunday afternoon break if a pub caused excessive noise, annoyance or disorder.

Most pubs in Bradford welcomed the change, which allowed them freedom of choice. Some landlords did not welcome the change, as they were forced to open by their breweries.

In April 2000 the government announced that pubs and shops would in future be able to sell alcohol round the clock, this being the most radical overhaul of licensing laws for forty years. The proposals aimed at modernizing regulations covering the sale of drink included sweeping away Sunday restrictions and giving children more access to pubs and bars.

The shake-up also included a crackdown on drink related crime. The police were given new powers to order immediate closure of rowdy premises. People convicted of violent behaviour in pubs could be banned for life from all premises. The landlords are able to apply for permission from local authorities, rather than magistrates, to sell alcohol up to 24 hours a day, 7 days a week.

Only time will tell if these new laws will affect the drinking habits of the townsfolk of Bradford.

> The Righteous Minds of Innkeepers
> Induce Them Now and Then
> To Crack a Bottle With a Friend
> Or Treat Unmoneyed Men.
>
> *G. K. Chesterton, 1874- 1936*

Bradford's Ale Brewers

Traditionally, estate workers could expect to receive free ale as part of their wages. Perhaps this happened at Barton Farm, when it was part of Shaftesbury Abbey's Monastic Estate. There was a malthouse and brewery at the Barton Farmhouse, which was situated near the well on the East Side of the house, near the granary.

An inventory of the Abbess of Shaftsbury's possessions at Barton Farm in 1367 showed the following: In the Brewhouse, 1 Vat and 1 Furnace. In the Malthouse, 2 Cribs for carrying malt, 1 Wooden Shovel for turning Malt, 1 Iron bound bucket with iron coterell for the well of the malthouse. Also listed were two keys and locks for the malthouse.

In 1392 repairs were needed in the malthouse when a mason spent 11 days remaking the walls around the great door arch. At the same time, a new trough was required for the brewery. Carpenters worked two days planing two large end boards, which then had to be taken to Shaftesbury, with a supply of lead, so that they could be made into the trough and lined with the lead. The completed trough was then transported back to Bradford. It was put back into place at the farm, and it took six more days for the masons to put a wall back around it.

During the renovation of the West Barn on this site in 2001, builders discovered a fireplace and kiln. They were clearing an area to build a car park. Archaeologists believe that this is the kiln which was used by workers in the beer-making process.

Up to about the 18th century the making of ale or beer was a recognized duty of the housewife, often referred to as 'ale-wives'. After the ale had been brewed they could sell and serve it from their home, or as it became known, the Alehouse.

It was not long before the Alehouse became known as the Public House, which was a contraction of 'Public Alehouse'. It is worth contrasting this with The Inn which, as well as providing food and beer, also provided accommodation for guests and stabling for horses.

By the 1780s beer began to be produced on a commercial scale by small local breweries. One of the town's earliest documented examples is that of Richard Pearce who bought the Maidenhead Inn premises and its own Malthouse at Bradford in 1755. It is believed that the Malthouse originated sometime before 1611. This is now the Bradford Town Club in Market Street.

This era saw the beginning of a steady increase in brewing commerce in Bradford. In 1822 John Spencer in Whiteheads Lane, and George Wilkins at the Seven Stars Inn Newtown, were both brewing beer. They were both to play a major role in the town's brewing industry for many years to come. (More on these local breweries later).

The records of the Bradford Union show that Emily Haxell of Bradford, was brewing ale, 'sometimes 2 days a week, sometimes 3'. We do not know if Emily continued brewing as by 10th October 1830,The Beer Retailers Act permitted any householder who wished to sell ale or beer and was eligible to pay poor rate, to do so by purchasing an excise licence for 2 guineas.

Trade directories inform us that in Bradford by 1838 there were 16 beer retailers and 18 pubs or inns, and by 1848 there were 18 Public Houses or Inns, 11 Beer Retailers and 6 Brewers/Maltsters in the town. These numbers stayed at roughly the same level throughout the rest of the 19th century.

The Sale of Beer Act of 1855 was introduced which closed Inns at 10pm on Sundays. About 150,000 people, who opposed the Act, rioted in Hyde Park, London on 1st July that year. It was reported that the police handled things badly, trying to drive a way through the crush with truncheons.

A Wine and Beer Act of 1869 was introduced, and at this time few beerhouses brewed their own beer and many were in the brewers' hands. With this Act came some measure of jurisdiction over beerhouses and this gave local Wiltshire Justices a degree of control over future licences.

A description of a typical Wiltshire Inn

Writing in 1875, Swindon-born Richard Jefferies, who wrote with great knowledge and a genuine love for Wiltshire folk life, made the following interesting commentary on the changing life of the late 19th century inn:

> 'The places where agriculturists and the principal inhabitants of the parish do meet together and discuss matters in a friendly spirit are the churchyard before the service, and the village Inn. The last has fallen into disuse. It used to be the custom to meet at the central Inn night after night to hear the news, as well as for convivial purposes. In those days of slow travelling and a few posts, the news was

communicated from village to village by pedlars, or carrier carts calling, as they went at each Inn. But now it is a rare thing to find farmers at the Inn in their own town. The old drinking habits have died out. It is not that there is any prejudice against the Inn; but there is a cessation of the inducement to sit there night after night. People do not care to drink as they used to, and they get the news just as well at home. The parlour at the Inn has ceased to be the village parliament.'[1]

Perhaps due to the effects of some of Jefferies' views on changing drinking habits, and in an effort to preserve a decent level of sales, brewers embarked on a wholesale acquisition of ale and beerhouses. By 1890 about 70% of alehouses were 'tied' to breweries.

In addition to this, Gladstone introduced his Inland Revenue Act of 1880, which directly taxed home brewing. It was not until 1963 – when this Act was replaced after a period of 83 years – that the custom of home brewing was released from taxation.

> No, Sir, Their is nothing which has yet been contrived by man, by which so much happiness is produced as by a good Tavern or Inn.
>
> *Samuel Johnson, 1776*

Inns, Hotels and Taverns

By the beginning of the 17th century inns were well adapted to the needs of their times. Historian Fynes Moryson, writing in 1617, gives a clear picture of their conduct and economy:

'As soon as a passenger comes to an Inn, the servants run to him, and one takes his horse, and walks him till he be cold, then rubs him and gives him food. Another servant gives the passenger his private chambers, and kindles his fire; a third pulls his boots and makes them clean. Then the host prepares his meal, which will cost him sixpence.'

This vivid 17th Century description bears witness to the fact that inns had no bars, no set dinner and no dining room. Guests had their meals served in their private room – or in the kitchen, depending on social standing. These changes did not appear regularly until later in the 18th century. Some Inns later adapted to the more modern 'Hotel' (or 'otels as the former Poet Laureate Sir John Bejteman so charmingly called them).

The intuitive reader can surmise that treatment by innkeepers varied considerably between those guests who rode inside the stagecoach, and those who did not.

Slowly 17th century alehouses grew less primitive, even though the main drinking room may still have been the kitchen, for warmth. Any furniture provided by the alehouse keeper was simple in design, with perhaps a basic trestle table and stools. However, drunkenness and the problems it caused to family life did not improve, and is well illustrated by the following extract from one anonymous writer in 1646:

' ... And who doth not see the Country Husbandman spend more time in these pestilent Ale-houses than he doth on the plough, and oft times runs so far on the score that he runs himself out of all, and then he, his wife and children must beg. Do but look on the tradesman, if many of them do not spend more time in the Ale-house than in their shops; and if a customer come to speak with him, his careful wife many times must hunt from ale-house to ale-house for her husband, and many times finds him speechless, and so hastens to beggary himself and his whole family.'

Our inns are scarcely public places in the sense that railway stations and libraries are, but they are partially public. We know they are commercial undertakings. The rules for proper behaviour in inns, published in a broadside in the 16th century, insist on the dignity of the innkeeper and respect due to his house:

'Our Saviour in the Gospel commends the use of inns. Yea, Christ himself by his own presence did sanctify the use of inns by eating his Passover there.

It must not be accounted a small matter to afford houseroom, lodging, rest and food to the comforts of God's children. Though your house, as an inn, be open for all men to come unto, yet account honest men your best guests. Because your guests be God's children, and their bodies the members of Christ, let their usage for meat, lodging, drink and sleep be such as becomes worthy personages. Content yourselves with an honest gain, so using your guests as

they may have an appetite to return to you when they are gone
from you.

And for the guests, use an inn not as your own house, not to
dwell in, but to test for such time as you have just and needful
occasion, and then to return to your own families. Eat and drink
for necessity and strength; not for lust. At table let your talk
be powdered with the salt of heavenly wisdom, as your meat is
seasoned with material and earthly salt. Above all, abhor all oaths,
cursing and blasphemy.'

I doubt if some customers in today's drinking places in Bradford have read
the above.

The 'Tavern' originally specialized in the sale of wine but the word
had by this time lost its original meaning, with the name being used as an
alternative to public house. The term 'pub' itself does not appear to have
been in general use until later in the 19th century.

17th Century Protests

In the early 17th century there were approximately a dozen alehouses
in Bradford. Things did not run too smoothly in the town, for in 1628 a
petition was presented to the Justices of the Peace meeting at the Quarter
Sessions in Devizes:

'The humble peticon of the inhabitants of Bradford, Wilts humblie
sheweth that there are within the towne of Bradford such a
company of ale-houses, and such alsoe that doe keepe disorder in
theire houses, not onely by entertaining poore workmen and day
labourers and sufferinge them to spend theire money when as their
wife and children are ready to starve and want of food, but also
suffering the sinn of drunkenness to be there daylie committed
as well in the tyme of Divine Service as also at other tymes, by
means whereof there often happeneth quarrellinge and fighting to
the great disturbance of the neighbours and the greate dishonour
of the Almighty God and the great impoverishment of the towne.
Wherefore we doe humbly desire that they may be all suppressed
by order of Sessions, there being an Inn and some other alehouses
besides, that are fit to give entertainment to Strangers. And we
shalbe ever bound to pray to God for all yor Worpps happines in
this life and endles Glorie in the World to come.' [2]

The petition is signed by six persons, including Robert Townsend and Thomas Mathew, who add 'gard' after their names. Little appeared to have happened following this petition, for in 1645/6 Bradford supplied a large quantity of beer to the Parliamentary Garrison at Great Chalfield.

Later in that century Bradford residents, with others in the county, presented a petition to the quarter sessions in 1682, which reads:

> 'We desire that this Court will order that noe Justice of the Peace in this county shall graunt lycence to any Ale House Keeper in this county unlesse they the said Ale House Keepers and every one of them doe first bring a certificate signed by the Minister and Church Wardens of the respective Parishes that they doe constantly frequent the Parish Church to heare Divine Service and receive the Sacrament.'[3]

Early Inn Survey

The first known survey of inns in the country was made in 1686. The Secretary of war needed to ascertain where troops might be billeted in the whole Kingdom. Disappointingly the inns are not named, we only know the number of beds and the stabling for horses. In Bradford the number of beds available was 102 and 54 stabling. This compared with 61 and 66 respectively for Trowbridge, and 52 and 64 for Corsham. In total Wiltshire compared very well with other counties at that time.

Sunday Tippling

The authorities were still being kept busy by the ale-house keepers in the town, for in 1724 Richard Gorton, ale-house keeper (site unknown) of Bradford was summoned through the constables and parish officers 'to show why he should not be fined 10 shillings (50p) for allowing drinking and tippling on the Lord's Day commonly called Sunday.'

In 1737 there is a report which tells us that the authorities swooped on 44 keepers of unlicensed alehouses in Bradford and fined them a total of £3.

In 1744 records show that one Bradford beerhouse keeper was fined for 'selling beer without licence, obstructing the constable, suffering "Tiplin" on the Lord's Day and swearing.'

Alehousekeeper Recognizance Licences

A Recognizance was a bond or obligation entered into before a magistrate to perform a specified act or fulfill a condition.

James I was a staunch upholder of Lenten fasting. In 1620 he introduced a proclamation to forbid the eating of meat during Lent and on every Friday in the year. All innholders and alehousekeepers were to enter into recognizances undertaking that they would not permit meat to be prepared or sold in their houses during Lent and serve no suppers on Fridays. Each Innholder bound him/herself in £10 and had to find two sureties of £5 each.

Records show that in Bradford the following entered into a recognizance in 1620:

'Adrian Cripps - Innkeeper, Sureties - Robert Parrishe, Butcher & Robert Coope, Glover, both of Bradford.
Robert Keare - Alehousekeeper, Sureties - Edward Hawkins, Baker & William Hayes, Carrier, both of Bradford.
John Dicke - Brewer, Sureties Robert Parrishe, Butcher & William Archard, Carrier, both of Bradford.
Jane Joanes - Alehousekeeper, Sureties - James Silvey, Broadweaver & Robert Titt, Tucker, both of Bradford.
William Baylie - Innkeeper, Sureties - John Houlton, Baker & Peter Godbye, Glover, both of Bradford.
John Dike - Beerbrewer, was one of the sureties for Robert Parishe (sic), Butcher.

Regrettably records do not indicate the address of these entries.

From around 1780-1830 alehouse keepers were required, when applying for a licence, to abide by the following conditions: 'No bear baiting, no gaming with cards on the part of apprentices, journeymen and similar common people, no harbouring of women of notoriously bad fame.'

Alehousekeeper Recognizance Licences inform us that 20 alehouses were licensed in the Bradford Hundred in 1780. Any of these could have bought their beer from local breweries.

An old West Country name for an unlicensed alehouse was 'Kidleywink'. In 1830 a gentleman suggested to the Chancellor of the Exchequer the idea of retail breweries. His name was Kidley Wink – hence the term Kidleywink as applied to the alehouses.

Bradford's Cider Maker

There is little evidence that cider was made in Bradford in great quantities. However, in July 1794, James Elliott of Bradford, Tripe Seller, was convicted before Thomas Bush, one of His Majesty's Justices of the Peace, at The New Bear, in the town. He was accused of selling 'Cyder' without a licence. He was ordered to forfeit 40 shillings, being the first offence, with costs of six shillings.

Ale Drinking Vessels

Today we drink our ale, or beer, mainly from tankards or glasses – very different from the drinkers of the seventeenth century. Thomas Heywood, writing in 1633, listed some of the vessels used in those times:

'Of drinking cups, divers and sundry sorts we need; some of elme, some of box, some of maple and holly. Mazers, Broadmouthed dishes, Naggins, Whiskins, Piggins, Creuzes, Ale-Bowles, Wassel-bowles, Court dishes, Tankards and Cannes, from a pottle (half-gallon) to a pint, from a pint to a gill. Other bottles of leather, for they are mostly used among syche characters as the shepherds and harvest people of the countrey; small jacks need like in many alehouses, tipt with silver. We need besides cups made of horns, of cokernuts, of goords, and of eggs of ostriches.'

The Toby Jug came later in the next century.

St George he was for England,
And before he killed the dragon
He drank a pint of English Ale
Out of an English flagon.

G.K. Chesterton, The Englishman, 1920

Bradford's Meeting Place

The *Bradford Pictorial Guide* of 1837 refers to the fact that:

'there were but few residents in the town who received a Daily newspaper, or even a weekly one in those days, being too expensive for the many. The traders of the town usually met together in what was called the "Tradesman's Room" at the Swan Inn, to hear the news and talk over the trade of the town, in a dreamy, sleepy kind of manner. Occasionally helping each other's observations by a pinch of snuff, a whiff of tobacco, or a sip of the celebrated Bradford XXX beer.'

Temperance Society

The British and Foreign Temperance Society was founded in 1821 in the hope of solving the country's drinking problem. In 1845 a Temperance Hall was erected in Sladesbrook, Bradford. At a meeting at the Temperance Hall in 1892, brother W. P. Hanny, who had just completed his 90th year and had been an abstainer for 60 years spoke on 'Things I remember in Bradford.' Referring to the town in the early 1800s, he stated:

'There were two water carts in the town, one took clean water to the brewery [Brewery unknown] to make beer, the other took dirty water to the mill to make wool clean.'

Mr Hanny went on to recall:

'one (unknown) Bradford Publican attempted to burn his house down by putting a red hot poker in the middle of a feather bed. However, the burning smell attracted attention. We don't know why he carried out this act, but the man was eventually tried, convicted and hung at Salisbury.'

Later, after its closure, the White Hart Inn building, situated at the junction of Silver Sreet and Market Street, which was later known as Knees Corner, was demolished and rebuilt by the Rev. Mr Thring. It opened in 1879 as a Temperance Hotel and included a coffee bar.

Temperance Hotels were places where teetotal sales representatives and other travellers could put up for the night in modest comfort without temptation or embarrassment.

Drunkenness

Despite the efforts of the Temperance Society, drunkenness still periodically caused problems in Bradford. A letter from a Ratepayer living in The Shambles to the *Wiltshire Times* in December, 1883 makes interesting reading:

'Sir
When the Town Commissioners purchased the Market, we were

given to understand it would be conducted on a better plan than it was before. I am sorry to say it is ten times worse. The Shambles was blocked for nearly two hours on Saturday night, and it was nearly impossible to pass. The cursing was something shameful to listen to. There were 2 or 3 notable characters that attended the market, they were near intoxicated, and they make the market unfit for decent people to attend. There seems to be no one with authority to stop them.'

Drunkenness wasn't confined to the general public. In April 1840 Captain Meredith, the first Chief Constable of Wiltshire, wrote that there had been frequent complaints of drunkenness in the force – particularly on payday:

'These occurrences are disgraceful to the Constables and discreditable to the Superintendents.' Abstinence was encouraged at every opportunity. It was a serious offence to be seen in a Public House while on duty. In June 1842 a constable was convicted of neglect of duty and disobedience of orders by drinking in a beerhouse in Wiltshire, when he should have been on duty. He was sent to Fisherton Gaol, Salisbury, for one month hard labour.

A drunken gathering (wood engraving by Thomas Bewick)

Introduction of Restaurant Facilities

In the late 1950s, it was thought that pubs should be made more pleasing to customers, and during the 1960s and 1970s many pubs developed restaurants or restaurant areas, the place for the best food at reasonable prices.

A further major change is that many pubs no longer have separate bar areas; the old distinction between public bars and lounge bars has almost entirely disappeared.

Jug and Bottle

For many years it was the custom for some families to buy their beer or ale from the 'Jug and Bottle' at their local pub. These were tiny serveries separate from the main bars, where take-away sales were made. This was also a vital part of every landlord's income. These 'Jug and Bottles' gradually disappeared from most pubs when supermarkets came along offering a wide range of cut price drinks in cans or non-returnable bottles.

Campaign for Real Ale: CAMRA

By 1974 the Campaign for Real Ale (CAMRA) was in full swing. Its aim is to promote real ale, which is brewed from traditional ingredients and allowed to mature naturally in the cask in the pub cellar and served without gas pressure. Most publicans in Bradford now offer at least one real ale for their customers' delectation.

Pub Entertainment

The long tradition of pub games has managed to continue with darts, skittles, shove ha'penny and pool. This has now grown to include modern electronic slot machines, juke boxes – not to mention video games. Publicans should be congratulated in taking the challenging step of re-introducing live music in the form of jazz, blues and traditional folk groups. Television is also laid on by many publicans in the town.

In the early 1930s the Mass Observation Society compiled a study of pub life. They found that most people went to the pub to drink, talk, think and smoke. They talked about sport, weather, betting, work, drinking, politics and sex. They also played games such as, cards, dominoes, darts, skittles, bar billiards and shove ha'penny, they also quarrelled and fought.

Even politics will get an airing, certainly at election time. Daniel Batchelor, a Bradfordian who had emigrated to America, wrote a long letter of reminiscence which was published in the *Wiltshire Times* in 1885. In his 'Reminiscences of Bradford 50 Years Ago by an Old Bradfordian in America' he refers to an election campaign fought some fifty years before:

'I think it must be nearly 50 years ago that some deft rhymster, posted in the Swan club room, at Bradford, an electioneering verse. The candidate to whom he referred had recently come down from London to Devizes where on the hustings he had been put in nomination as M.P. for North Wiltshire, Sir John Cam Hobhouse having previously nominated Paul Methuen, who was detained at home by illness.

The town was divided in sentiments for separate candidates. William Hale, at the Swan, Alex Wilkins, at the Seven Stars, John Dory, at the Bell, Hunt, at the Royal Oak, were among the stoutest advocates of Methuen. The other hostelries were about equally divided, save the portly John Kittlety, at Woolley, was conspicuous in person and power for the blues [opposition]. At the Old Bear Jim Whitaker and Cobbler White held high converse over the affairs of the county, while at the New Bear tap-room a jolly set was led by Jim Cash.'

Anecdotes of the Pub Landlord in Bradford

The Pub Landlord has, all through the ages, adapted himself to all types of customer. An early 20th century writer stated:

'He must be silent with the silent, and chatty with the chatty. He must be able to talk to the sportsman, the shopkeeper, the lord, the amateur politician, the lawyer, the stockbroker, the old man, the dashing youth, the lonely lady, the facetious man, the gloomy man, the pompous man; and must be able to make each believe that he is interested in them. He may have a delightful pub or inn, wonderfully furnished, excellent cook and service; but if he himself is not a pleasant person, these things will count for nothing.'[4]

In one public house in Bradford before the Second World War, the publican displayed a small box by the side of the door saying, 'Please take one.' The box contained a number of cards, bearing the name and sign of the pub, with the message, 'You're no Adonis, but we'd love to see your face again.' Another pub displayed a notice, 'Please don't leave your glasses on the seats. It's bad for my glasses and your seat!'

Talking to a landlord, post-second world war, on the subject of his profession, he humorously commented:

'To obtain a licence is a hard task. A discharged lunatic's the only man who holds an official certificate of sanity. The publican's the only man who holds an official certificate of absolute straight character. He's got to have one or he'd never be allowed to have a pub.'

On a more serious note he carried on to say:

'An expectant publican has to obtain a letter from three householders of good standing, who state that they have known him for five years, and that to their knowledge, his character is unassailable. Before he makes his application he must send notice, with the three letters, to the Superintendent of Police. When the Superintendent has made full enquiries upon these letters, and upon anything arising from them, he must appear before the Justices for cross examination. He must also produce references, apart from the householders' letters, showing what his previous occupations have been and his behaviour in them; these must be without blemish.'

> I feel no pain, dear mother, now
> But oh! I am so dry!
> Oh, take me to a Brewery,
> And leave me there to die.
>
> *Anon.*

'ALES'

From its earliest times the Christian Church has decorated its calendar with feast days in celebration of Saints, a particular time of the year or to raise funds for the church, seasonal feasts being a hangover from the sowing and reaping festivities of heathenism. Like the drinks consumed, these convivialities were known as 'Ales' and were called Bride-Ales, Easter-Ales, Whitsun-Ales, Christmas-Ales and Church Ales etc.

They were frowned on by Puritan Philip Stubbs, writing in 1583:

'In certain townes where dronken Bacchus bears swaie, against Christmas and Easter, Whitsuntide or some other time, the churchwardens of every parishe provide half a score or twentie quarters of mault, whereof some they buy of the church stocke and some is given them of the parishioners themselves, everye one conferring somewhat, according to his abilities; which adult being made into very strong beere or ale, is sette o sale, either in the church or some other place assigned to that purpose. Then when this is set abroche, well is he that can get the soonest to it, and spend the most at it. In this kind of practice they continue six weeks, a quarter year, yea, halfe a year together. That money, they say, is to repair their churches and chappels with, to buye books for service, cuppes for the celebration of the sacrement, surplesses for St John, and other necessaries, and they maintain extraordinary charges in their parish besides.'

Another contemporary, Thomas Percival, wrote, 'Keapinge of Church Ales, in which with leapinge, dansinge and kyssnge, they maynteyne the profett of their church.'

25

In Bradford these 'ales' were held at Church House, Church Street and although these gatherings were often 'jolly rowdy occasions', I have found no evidence that Percival's description of the 'goings on' occurred in Bradford.

The final word on these ales is written adequately by Peter Mews in his 'Ex-ale-tation' of ale in 1671:

> The Churches much owe, as we all do knowe,
> For when they be drooping and ready to fail.
> By Whitsun or Church ale up again they shall go,
> And owe their repairing to a pot of good ale.

Various governments tried for hundreds of years to put a stop to these ales, but with the support of the church, which profited by them, they managed to survive until their final suppression by Oliver Cromwell.

In Conclusion

Richard Jefferies writing on the subject of the village pub in 1889 stated the following:

> 'You pass a public house in the summer's evening. You see a number of men grouped about trestle-tables out of doors, and others sitting at the open window; there is an odour of tobacco, a chink of glasses and mugs. You can smell the tobacco and see the ale; you cannot see the indefinite power, which holds men there – the magnetism of company and conversation.'[5]

Most visitors to our shores, when asked what they most like about this country; would answer 'your Inns and Pubs.' We sometimes take them for granted, but they are unique to us and are among our greatest assets. Nowhere is the spirit of Great Britain better expressed; they are a continuing thread through our social history, representing stability, as long as they are still there, things aren't so bad. British life and leisure and a spirit of the traditional country pub still flourishes in Bradford.

The Seven Stars, Newtown: Public House and Brewery

An early Seven Stars Inn site, now 19 Newtown (formerly No. 71) can be traced back as a property to at least 1722, when the owner was Paul Methuen, Clothier, and his tenant was Thomas Ferrett. By 1748 the property was leased to one Thomas Merrick.[1]

An interesting attachment to an Assignment of Mortgage has been found dated 10th March 1749, which tells us of Thomas Merrick who was the Victualler at the Seven Stars Inn. This states that his new dwelling house was part stone-tiled and part thatched. It gave a property value not exceeding £120. The value of his stock, liquor and casks in trade did not exceed £80. This made a grand total of £200.[1]

The inn was leased to John Sandell, who was Thomas Merrick's son-in-law in 1773, thus continuing the family link by marriage.

Between 1782 and 1789 the rateable value of the property increased, and this suggests considerable development of the site. It is probable that Sandell started to improve the facilities, and this may have included the construction of the malthouse, which adjoined the west side of the inn.[1]

One account from October 1793 tells us of John Sandell submitting details to the Excise Officers at Bradford. This detail shows:

1 Malthouse, 1 Cistern, 1 Couch, 2 floors for Couching, 1 kiln, 2 rooms for storing of dry barley and malt. ('Couch' means to spread grain on a floor to germinate).[2]

The *Universal British Directory* of 1793-8 confirms his trade as a Maltster.

In 1794 Sandell's daughter Grace married James Wilkins, and by 1804 Wilkins was in occupation at The Seven Stars building, with his father-in-law John Sandell still occupying the malthouse.

On John Sandell's death c.1817, Grace and James Wilkins inherited the Seven Stars, and their son Alexander was granted his first licence at the Inn in the latter part of 1824, and he built a brewery on a 'confined site' behind the Inn which he had purchased by 1841.[2] It was on this site that he brewed

PICKWICK BREWERY.

WILKINS BROS & HUDSON LTD,

BREWERS,
WINE & SPIRIT MERCHANTS,
MALTSTERS,

AND PICKWICK BREWERY, CORSHAM, WILTS.

TELEPHONE Nº
BRADFORD-ON-AVON 3.
CORSHAM 46Y.

TRADE   MARK

Bradford on Avon.

24 Jany 1912

the popular XXXX beer.

Initially the Wilkins family malted and brewed purely for sale in The Seven Stars. Trade must have developed well, for between 1859-64 they built the large brewery almost opposite the pub in Newtown, replacing the houses there.[1] At first this was known as The Seven Stars Brewery, later the Newtown Brewery, and at its closure the Pickwick Brewery.

Following the death of Alexander Wilkins in 1862 (aged 61) his sons James Alexander Wilkins, Henry Sandell Wilkins and William Wilkins, became owners, to be known as 'Messrs. Wilkins Bros'. The family business continued its growth to the extent that Henry Sandell Wilkins was elected President of the Bradford Licensed Victuallers Association somewhen before 1878.[4] By 1881 ten men and two boys were employed at the brewery.[1]

The Wilkins family scrap book of the time has an entry which recalls the time of the 'Great Floods' in Bradford. One of the family wrote of an incident on 23rd/24th October 1882, which related to one of the Wilkins Bros horses drowning at Bathford, due to the negligence of the driver (named Wilkins). He allowed the horse to pass through the ford when in a state of flood.

Another contrasting tale was copied from the back of the scrap book Re: Wilkins Bros brewery:

'August 17th 1889. The first of what is intended to be an annual excursion came off on Saturday, when through the kindness of the partners Messrs. H S Wilkins & E Poulter, the employees of the brewery and their wives to the number of about 50, were treated to a trip to Weymouth. The weather on the whole was very fine and the day was thoroughly enjoyed.'[2]

In 1890 the brewery, malthouses and yards were mortgaged by Walter Wilkins and Wm. Wilkins. One can speculate that Messrs. Wilkins financially overstretched themselves at this time, due to the ownership of stock and a great deal of property in Trowbridge, Bradford and Bath in 1889.[1]

On 29th September 1890 a fire insurance policy was taken up to cover the Seven Stars Inn. This also covered the brewery, malthouse and store

Opposite top: Letterhead of Wilkins Brothers and Hudson's Pickwick Brewery

Opposite centre: Wilkins Brothers and Hudson's delivery lorry, circa 1912

Opposite bottom:Wilkins brewery workers posing for the camera at the works in Newtown, an imposing building now converted into apartments

rooms on the inn side of Wine Street. The tenant at that time was one Bainton.[3]

At a special meeting of the Bradford Licensed Victuallers Association it was unanimously resolved to record the great loss which had been sustained by the death of their President Mr Henry Sandell Wilkins, who died on 7th November 1896, aged 67. He had occupied the position since the formation of the Association upwards of 18 years previously.[5]

Within a few months articles of association were drawn up stating that a new company would be formed called Wilkins Bros & Hudson Ltd.[2]

The Hudson family are thought to have owned the brewery at the former White Lion Inn, now 38 & 39 Newtown, and another at the Mason's Arms in Newtown.[1] They lived at Lynchetts in Woolley Street, Bradford.[4]

The formation was completed on 14th May 1897[6], when Mr Walter James Wilkins became Chairman – a position he maintained until the brewery was 'absorbed' by Ushers in 1920.[2]

A new mash tun was added to the brewery and, in 1896, shortly following the formation of the new company, a covered iron footway was built across Wine Street to convey the wort from the brewery to the malthouse. The bridge was approximately 18 foot 6 inches long. and 7 foot 6 inches high, and was designed to carry 4 tons.[6]

More changes followed a board meeting in 1905, when the brewery name was changed from Newtown Brewery Bradford, to Pickwick Brewery. It was owned in conjunction with the Pickwick Brewery at Corsham.[5]

Things did not always run smoothly for the brewery and, at a meeting of the Bradford Council's Highway Committee on 26th April 1906, a letter from Mrs L. Colhoun was read by the Clerk complaining of the smoke from Messrs. Wilkins chimney in Newtown. At a later meeting the Chairman read a letter from Mr W.J. Wilkins:

'We are most anxious to cause as little annoyance as possible to residents near the brewery and we have endeavoured to lessen smoke with some success. When a limit has been fixed by the Council as to the time of day allowed for the emission of black smoke from ALL the chimneys in the town, our firm will be pleased to fall in line. The brewery has been in existence for something over 100 years, and surely in selecting a residence within a short distance from so large a chimney the possibility of a nuisance from the same should be taken into consideration. A great quantity of steam is required in a brewery and unfortunately it is impossible to produce the same without smoke.'[7]

The Council did not feel it necessary to take the matter further.

In the 4th February 1915 edition of the *Devizes & Wiltshire Gazette* we are shown the generosity of Messrs. Wilkins Bros & Hudson, when they sent a gift of a nine- gallon cask of beer to be consumed by 'Inmates' at the Avoncliff workhouse at Christmas 1914.

However, on 30th July 1915 Frederick John Young, licensee of The Seven Stars, Newtown was summoned before Bradford Police court for selling a pint of beer in an unsealed vessel to Lucy Bancroft, a girl under 14 years of age. He was fined 5 shillings (25p).[8]

Above: Sketch of the Seven Stars Inn
Below: Advertisement from a town directory of 1891. Seven stars may still be seen above the gate at the entrance to the former brewery

Mr William Wilkins, one of the founders of the firm of Wilkins Bros & Hudson Ltd. of Newtown Brewery, died in February 1917. He had taken over his father's business as a brewer, maltster and farmer many years earlier. He retired from the brewery about thirty years previously.[2]

The growth of Wilkins Bros & Hudson Ltd. continued steadily during the early part of the 20th century, with their acquisition of properties throughout the West Country, examples of which included not only those in Bradford but also those at Bath and in Trowbridge. Despite this, a decision was made during 1919 to sell the company to Ushers brewery of Trowbridge, which took place on 23rd February 1920. The following Bradford holdings were transferred to Ushers[2]:

Pickwick Brewery, Newtown (Formerly known as the Newtown brewery).

The Seven Stars Inn, including the Cottage at 20 Newtown which was then being used as a grocer's shop adjoining the east side of the Seven Stars Inn.

The Bell Inn, including adjacent cottage, and the site of 3 cottages in the rear.

The Rising Sun, Winsley Road.

The King's Head Inn, Whitehill.

The cottages at Wine Street - Nos 1, 2, 3 & 15.

Premises formerly known as the Royal Oak, The Shambles, then used as an eating house and barber's shop.

The Three Horseshoes Inn, including a cottage used as a Cobbler's shop, adjoining the inn on the south side.[8]

Following this merger Mr Gilbert Hudson, a partner in the old established brewery firm of Wilkins Bros & Hudson Ltd, became a Director of Ushers Brewery. He died in March 1933, aged 59 years.[2]

Following the sale, Ushers made adjustments to their properties, one of which was demolition work to the rear of the Seven Stars Inn.

The late Jack Stafford, who lived and worked in Bradford all his life in the building industry, recalls details of the demolition work in the late 1920s/early 1930s, which included part of the Seven Stars Brewery in Newtown. This site was situated immediately behind, and also on the same side of Wine Street as the Seven Stars Inn.

The contractor, Mr Austin (who had a workshop in Whiteheads Lane) thought this a dangerous site to erect scaffolding for demolition due to the narrowness of the road and the rather acute bend at the bottom of Wine Street.

A man named Dagger, a plasterer and tiler who worked for Mr Austin, was dismantling the building from the inside. He piled the stones on the wooden floor of the top storey in the several floored building. At one point the weight of the stones was too much for the floor and they crashed down through each floor to the ground. Dagger just managed to jump onto a secure wall and escaped unhurt. Sudden death being fortunately avoided![9]

After the end of the Second World War the use of the brewery site was ended, but was utilized by various local industries, including Enfield Cycle Co., H.S. Long & Son and Berkeley Long.[10] In the 1960s Avon Rubber also used part of the site for the storage of rubber components.

Conversion of the site into office and residential accommodation was begun in 1991.[1]

Directors from Ushers agreed to sell the Seven Stars Inn on 3rd April 1969,[10] and this important part of Bradford's history, finally closed its doors to the public on 27th May 1969.

Spencer's Brewery

An early mention of Spencer's Brewery in Bradford was in a Trade Directory of 1822, when John Spencer was specified as a Common Brewer, trading at Whiteheads Lane.[1] John Spencer & Co. were also brewing in Silver Street in 1830[2], and John Spencer, owned the New Bear Inn by 1832.[3]

By 1838, according to another Trade Directory, John Spencer was joined by George and Thomas Spencer who were listed as brewers and maltsters, in Whiteheads Lane.[4] Interestingly, by 1841 a malthouse which operated in Frome Road, Bradford and was then owned by George and Thomas Spencer and John Spencer was omitted.

The malthouse is now commemorated in the name of the flats located on the same site, called the Maltings.[5]

The Spencer Brothers' trade grew so that they maintained their position as one of the two principal breweries in the town. The other being Wilkins

Short particulars and description.	Date of Conveyance to G. & T. Spencer's Brewery, Ltd., containing full description.
12. THE CROWN INN, Bathford, Somerset containing 1r. 24p. more or less	20th August, 1889.
13. A PERPETUAL YEARLY rent charge of 17/- payable by the Company of proprietors of the Kennett & Avon Canal	31st December, 1889.
14. THE WHITE HORSE INN, Twerton on Avon, with the garden messuage and hereditaments adjoining or belonging thereto	25th September, 1890.
15. THE PLOUGH INN with the garden Orchard and outbuildings thereto belonging situate at Bradford Leigh in the Parish of Bradford on Avon	30th September, 1889.
16. THE NEW INN, Westwood, Wilts, with the two cottages and gardens adjoining	23rd April, 1896.
17. THE ELY ARMS INN, Wroughton, Wilts, with gardens, Barn, Club room and closes of land adjoining containing 2a. 2r. 19p.	28th May, 1897.
18. THE LATE LAMB INN (formerly The Scribling Horse Inn), Bradford on Avon Together with the Brewhouse, Outhouse, messuage or dwellinghouse and other buildings and the pieces of ground adjoining or belonging thereto	31st July, 1889
19. THE FORGE HAMMER INN, Moorfields St. George, Bristol, with the cottage behind and the building, stable & yard opposite	9th October, 1889.
20. THE LATE ANGEL INN, Marshfield, with the garden, buildings and premises thereto belonging	26th February, 1891.
21. THE STAR INN, Bathford	3rd March, 1891.
22. THE DOG & FOX INN, Ashley Road, Bradford on Avon	24th July, 1891.

Above: Section of a list of properties sold by Spencer's Brewery to Usher's of Trowbridge; note Bradford on Avon pubs nos. 15, 18 and 22.

Opposite: Spencer's invoice listing items supplied and their cost

Bradford Brewery,

Bradford-on-Avon, Wilts.

Mr F Lane

To G & T Spencer's Bry

Limited.

TELEPHONE 20.

1911					
May 1	To Goods		3	4	6
5	" "		3	3	.
8	" "		2	15	6
12	" "		2	8	.
13	" "			12	.
17	" "		1	16	.
19				17	6
20			1	4	.
24			1	4	.
25			2	11	.
29			1	12	.
31			1	4	.
			22	11	6
			1	2	6
			21	9	.
			2	4	6
			19	4	6

629   June 12 1911

RECEIVED on account of

G. & T. Spencer's Brewery Ltd.

The sum of

£19 : 4 :

Dis for Cash 1. 2. 6

No discount allowed after
15th of this month.
Re Pulling Down Wall

& Co. This expansion in trade saw their ownership of both the Barge Inn at Frome Road (licensee William Henry Sainsbury) and the New Bear, in Silver Street (licensee Ann Mundy) in 1841.[6] Within a few months George, Thomas and John also included a house and garden in addition to the New Bear Inn, the Barge Inn and the brewery and malthouse amongst their properties.[7]

In 1851 George and Thomas Spencer were Master Brewers employing 16 men, of whom George Rawlings and Henry Nutt were both employed as Maltster Journeymen at Spencers' Frome Road malthouse. George Spencer was listed as being unmarried, but by 1861 this fact had changed and he was resident at St Margaret's Street with his wife and child and two servants. Harrods 1865 Directory lists William Chivers, brewer, in Whiteheads Lane.

During the ensuing years the Town Improvement Commissioners had been struggling with the danger of the irregular nature of the buildings in Silver Street. In 1883 two cottages (at Nos. 17 & 18 – next to Taylor's Wine Merchants) were demolished. This made way for G. & T. Spencer's new premises being built in 1884. A simple Spencer's inscription was positioned over the archway which is situate opposite The Bunch of Grapes, which can still be seen today.

G. & T. Spencer's Brewery was incorporated into a limited company on 5th April 1889 at a Directors' meeting at the Royal Hotel, Bath. Mr F. Ferris was elected Chairman and Mr Stephen Tryon was appointed Secretary.[8] The company bought the Lamb Inn, Bridge Foot by auction, on 5th June 1889 for £1,890, and let it to a Mr Hughes at a £50 quarterly tenancy. In July they also purchased the Rose and Crown, Mill Street, Bradford (price unknown) and the Plough Inn, Bradford Leigh for £900, in October 1889.[9] The original Bradford brewery in Whiteheads Lane was managed by Mr W.T. Knapp in 1890, and was replaced by A.D. Hatch in 1892 who remained in post until at least 1895.[10]

The company was still expanding and they acquired the Dog & Fox, Ashley, Bradford in March 1892 for £480.[8] By February 1896 Spencer's had also bought the malthouse and premises in Church Street, Bradford. They leased this to James Daris Taylor at a fixed rent of £18 a year.They bought the Queen's Head, Bradford on 28th October 1897.[8]

An excise licence was granted in February 1905 to G. & T. Spencer's Ltd. Bradford, in the name of A.D. Hatch, who had advanced to Managing Director of the firm. On 12th April 1905 he also applied for and was granted an additional excise licence to sell spirits (to be consumed off the premises) from the brewery.[10] By 1909 a Mr. W.M. Mitchell was brewery manager at 19, Whiteheads Lane.[11]

The licence for the Lamb Inn, Bridge Foot, was not renewed in May 1911. The premises were subject to annual flooding from the river Avon, and business was small. The building was in a bad state of repair and there were no stabling facilities. The Inn was closed in 1912, with Frederick Lane as the last licensee.[10]

The company let the empty Lamb Inn on 19th September 1912, as a common lodging house at a rent of £16.[8]

From this time onward Spencers' position as one of the significant brewers in the town dwindled to such an extent that at an extraordinary general shareholders meeting of 14th January 1914 at the Albion Chambers, Bristol, the Chairman moved and seconded by Mr B.D. Pope stated that:

'The company be wound up voluntarily and that Stephen Tryon of Albion Chambers, Bristol, Chartered Accountant be hereby appointed liquidator for the purposes of such winding up.'[8]

Following this decision there was a Sale by Auction at the Swan Hotel, Bradford in 1914:

Lot No. 1 – Spencers brewery, Whiteheads Lane, and Silver Street together with horizontal steam engine, Lancaster boiler and main shafting and gearwork, boiler house and washing shed, with a 2-storey building in the rear. Chimney shaft and the main building of 4-floors, comprising the brewery with extensive cellarage - also stone built and tiled dwelling house adjoining the brewery used as a Managers residence.[11]

Lot No. 2 – Also walled garden.[11] This may have been called 'The Close'.[11]

Lot No. 3 – Yard, buildings, comprising range of stabling for 5 horses also wagon shed and open shed. pump and well of water.[11]

Lot No. 4 – Paddock at top of Whiteheads Lane being number 222 on the Tithe Map. (Approx. over 1 acre). With stone built and slated stable.[11]

Lot No. 5 – Building of 2 floors situated in Silver Street. Beer cellars and drill hall.[11]

Lot No. 6 – Shop and premises being No. 1 St. Margarets Street, now in the occupation of Mrs Matilda Bartnett on a quarter tenancy.[11]

Also the premises adjoining, No. 2 St Margarets Street, including cellars, brewery store room and dwelling house[9] formerly the Queen's Head Inn, but now used as a cycle shop by Mr Charles Perkins on a fortnightly tenancy. Also shop and premises adjoining being no. 3 St Margaret's Street, now in the occupation of Mr J Mitchell on a weekly tenancy of (gross annual rental of £34.18s.0d).[11]

Lot no. 7 – Stone built and tiled shop, with stables and yard adjoining lot 6 now in the occupation of Mr. Albert Davis, together with the workshop over same in the occupation of Mr. Ben Crook, plumber and gas fitter. (Annual rental of lot 7 = £17).[11]

Ushers Brewery of Trowbridge were the successful purchasers of the above Lots, also sold to Ushers were the following Bradford properties:

G. & T. Spencer's Ale & Porter Stores (now partly the Ale & Porter restaurant) in Silver Street. A keystone in an adjacent building features Bacchus, God of Wine, plus his attendants Satyr and Silenus and partner Ariadne.

New Bear Hotel, Silver Street

The Barge Inn, Frome Road

The Beehive Inn, formerly the New Inn, Widbrook

The Stable, coach house and store rooms, with malthouse, malt kiln in the rear, Church Street, Bradford

The Plough Inn, Bradford Leigh.

The late Lamb Inn (formerly the Scribbling Horse Inn, Bradford), brewhouse, outside messuage & dwelling house

Dog and Fox Inn, Ashley Road

The Old Bear Inn, Silver Street, Bradford [all 11]

The brewery manager's house in Whiteheads Lane is now used as the Friends Meeting House[13]

In the late 1950s Eric Griffin and Gordon Fudge took over the Spencer's site for their burgeoning engineering company to be known as Griffin & Fudge. In the interim period after the First World War the old Spencer's buildings were used for several purposes, one of which was as storage facilities for the local rubber company. Messrs. Griffin & Fudge rarely used the top two storeys themselves due to unsafe conditions, and these floors were later demolished. However, there is pictorial evidence of the original large 4-storey building, from an aerial photograph of 1939. This also shows another 4-storey windowed building still standing, which is to the west side of Whitehead's Lane, and which was also part of the brewery works.[12]

The King's Arms and Brewery

Until very recently, a hand-painted plaque by the side door of the former public house situated on the corner of Coppice Hill and Silver Street, now the King's Spice Indian restaurant, mentioned that it was established in 1684. However, it was once The George and a Manorial Court record (The Court Baron) shows a change in ownership of a tenement next to The George, near the High Cross, at the slightly earlier date of 1678.

1888

KING'S ARMS BREWERY,

BRADFORD-ON-AVON.

E. HOLE,

LICENSED BREWER,

Is now open to Supply the Trade

WITH

BEER, ALE, OR PORTER,

IN ANY SIZED CASK.

THE "ONE-SHILLING" ALE

ESPECIALLY RECOMMENDED FOR FAMILIES,

Is sent out in $4\frac{1}{2}$, 9, 18, and 36 Gallon Casks.

SUPERIOR ALES

Brewed from the purest Malt and Hops only,
from 1s. 4d. to 1s. 8d. per Gallon.

ORDERS BY POST PUNCTUALLY ATTENDED TO.

The pub has changed its name several times over the centuries. We know this because there is a 1729 mortgage for the property decribing it as 'formerly called by the name of The Boot and now the George Inn'. By 1740 its name had changed to the New White Hart Inn.[1]

In 1808 John Bains was in occupation of the newly named King's Arms. (Where he remained until 1838, when for a brief period of three years Henry Brook took over; he was later elected to the Town Commissioners). In 1816 a former malthouse, buildings and house in Coppice Hill were sold. It is quite likely that Bains took up tenure of this Coppice Hill site for brewing purposes, due to its close proximity to his pub.[2]

In 1841 began the longest known occupation of the site by the Hole family, headed by Richard, who ran the business as the innkeeper. His prosperity allowed him the luxury of employing four servants by 1851, including Thomas Yeats as a brewer.

His wife Elizabeth Hole took over as innkeeper on Richard Hole's death in 1853. She continued until 1890, when her son Alfred H. Hole took over for five years until 1895. Alfred had been a proficient brewer in the family business since at least 1881, along with his sister Julia, who assisted her mother as Licensed Victualler.

William B. Harding replaced Alfred Hole as innkeeper and brewer in 1895. Harding's Brewery was situated behind and beside the King's Arms. This is indicated by the now fading inscription 'Harding's & Co. Ltd. Brewery' above an archway of the red brick building on the right side of the pub, which is now called Scrine's Chemist, 6 Silver Street. A 1901 advertisement placed by Harding stated that they were brewers of the celebrated 'Bravon' Ales and Stouts.

On 12th April 1905 the Public House Licensing Committee granted a licence to Edward Anthony Ruddle, of the firm of Simeon Ruddle & Son, Brewers, Bradford, for the sale of spirits to be consumed off the premises.[3] This is probably the first evidence of Ruddle's brewery in Bradford. Within a year, by April 1906, Ruddle received a complaint from Bradford's ratepayers association stating that the brewery chimney was causing excessive smoke nuisance. Receiving no reply, the Urban District Council requested that he abate the problem immediately. This is early evidence of the increased awareness of air pollution in Bradford.[4]

By 1907 Edward Ruddle brought in the services of William Broad Harris as Landlord of The King's Arms.[5] The brewery, by 1911 had changed its official name to the Bravon Brewery, although I gather the townsfolk still referred to it as Ruddles Brewery.[6]

Following the Military Services bill of January 1916, which compelled

Pre-1914 advertisement for the King's Arms, here styling itself as a hotel

The King's Arms, no longer brewing its own beers, but importing them from Usher's in Trowbridge

single men between the ages of 18-40 years to join the military forces, tribunals were set up to consider cases of men who considered themselves in essential occupations, and might therefore avoid enrolment. During one such tribunal Edward A. Ruddle, aged 36 years, was given six months exemption as he would have to close his brewery if enrolled.[7]

Edward Ruddle moved to No. 7 Silver Street by 1918 (recently Goodall's shop) Mr Goodall demolished the brewer's house before building his own shop.[8] Ruddle had previously spent at least ten years at 14 Coppice Hill.

We are told that the Ruddles brewery behind the King's Arms in Coppice Hill remained fully operational until at least 1923. Beer and ale could be seen steaming in 'boilers'. After brewing, horse drawn carts pulled up in Silver Street. When opening the large wooden doors, the carts were backed into the loading bay, and up to the wooden staging all around. The loading bay was located inside what is now Scrines' Chemist and Growing Needs (Nos 6 & 6A Silver Street).[8,9,10]

George Maslin's father used two mules and a cart to take full barrels of beer from the brewery to Stamper's Garage area for storage (near Westbury House).[2] As you walked along the pavement in Silver Street you could smooth the noses of the mules as they patiently waited for their load.[10]

With reference to the same subject, Jack Stafford relates that several blank windows in the building were possibly used as brewery offices, and are still to be seen in Coppice Hill, behind the King's Arms, where the high chimney was visible all around the town.[10]

A curious incident happened at 9.00 a.m on the morning of 22nd April 1926 concerning a lorry driven by A.F. Storer of London. He swerved just before reaching Mr Christopher's shop (29 Silver Street, now Davies Estate Agents) Apparently, a horse-drawn vehicle emerged from Kingston Road, and, to avoid a collision, Mr Storer swerved to the right, hoping to get a block on the curb. Unfortunately the pathway was lowered at the entrance to the Bravon brewery, and the lorry skidded on the greasy road, mounting the pavement. It ran full tilt into the side of the refreshment house occupied by Mrs Green[5] – now Tillions, 6a The Shambles.

By 1927 Mrs Alice Atkinson was landlady at The King's Arms, which seems to have been run as a completely separate business from that of the Brewery site in Coppice Hill. No mention of the Ruddles brewery was made; it does not appear in any of the directories of that time either, and we can find no further evidence of its existence as a brewery. 25 Coppice Hill is now called 'The Old Brewhouse'.

In June 1994 the Magic Pub Company bought the King's Arms property, and renovated the interior. In February 1995 it was re-opened as The Sprat

& Carrot. The Sprat & Carrot closed down during April 1998 when it was found the pub was infested with death watch beetle.

Following extensive repairs and redecoration internally and externally, the pub was re-opened on 21st November 1998, reverting back to its original name of the King's Arms. The new landlady, Nikki Bell, welcoming back old customers to the listed building.

However, its days as a pub were numbered: it latterly became a restaurant offering Mediterranean cuisine until its most recent incarnation in 2011 as an Indian restaurant known as King's Spice.

Other Malthouses and Breweries

As mentioned above, over the centuries malting and brewing on a small scale was carried out all over the town.

An early indenture of 1681 refers to Francis Yerbury of Bradford, Maltster, relating to tenements in Pippit Street and Church Street.[1] Later the Yerbury family, who were one of the prominent clothier families in the town, were still involved in malting for, in 1709, Francis Yerbury described himself as 'Maltster of Wellclose House, Bradford'.[2] John Yerbury, son of Francis, was shown as a Maltster in an exchange of land in 1719.[3] By 1737 the Yerburys had moved to Belcombe Brook House (now Belcombe Court), where 'improvements to the house made the site more commodious to the trade, the presence of water made it possible that the trade was either brewing or cloth manufacture', maybe both.[4]

A deed of exchange in 1716 between Edward Thresher, clothier of Bradford and John Whatley, Maltster also of Bradford, related to land in St Margaret's Street in the town.[5] A further deed dated 1729 states that Ebenezor Plurrett and Mary Tidcombe rented property for one year to James Collins, Maltster. This is the same property mentioned in an indenture of March 1735, which refers to a malthouse and brewhouse in St Margaret's Street. This is the land on which part of the present United Reform Church now stands.[5] In the Alehouse Applications of 1737 a Richard Chubb, Innholder is listed, and a Deed of Sale of this time also mentions Chubb in this area.[6] It is uncertain where his alehouse was situated. Either at the Fisherman Inn in the Square, St Margaret's Hill, or the Greyhound Inn also in St Margaret's Hill, but nearer to the main road – both in close proximity to the malthouse and brewery.

During 1736, Thomas Smith (who was described as being infirm) and Thomas Stephens, both maltsters of Bradford, served as Jurors at the Wiltshire Quarter Sessions of that year. Unfortunately it is not known where they plied their trade.

Sometimes the brewing process was completed in private houses and at farms such as William Applegate's farm at Widbrook. This farmhouse was built in 1834/5 for the Earl of Manvers estate and included a kitchen, brewhouse and dairy.[7] Malting and brewing continued in this way in the town throughout the 18th and early 19th century. By 1838 William Coles the Ironfounder was also malting at his premises in Trowbridge Road[8] (now No. 43 Trowbridge Road).

Thomas Ball Silcock was the owner of the complex by 1870, and he sold it to George Milsom, for the sum of £523.[1] The sale included the House, Foundry, Workshops, Gardens, Malthouse, Kiln and Stables.

The small brewers and maltsters survived and indeed prospered in the second half of the 18th century. However it was the age of the Industrial Revolution in Britain and the heyday of commercial brewers who produced beer and ale in larger quantities and better quality. The larger brewers began to own public houses as well, to guarantee an outlet for their products.

It was also the age of the stagecoach which, though relatively short, had a profound effect on Bradford. Coaching inns were established in the town (more later) as staging posts along the main routes to provide changes of horses, food, drink and accommodation. Stagecoach passengers were divided into those who travelled, more expensively, inside the coach and those who, more uncomfortably, rode on top or 'outside'. While the 'outsiders' were thought of as customers for the inn's only bar-room, the 'insiders', who had more money, were invited into the innkeepers private parlour or salon (later saloon).

Church Street Malthouse

During the mid-19th century Thomas Wheeler was malting in Church Street and Pippet Street[8], probably in the same premises that Francis Yerbury used in 1681 and referred to earlier. Previously the building had been used as a Poorhouse.[9] G. & T. Spencer bought the Church Street Malthouse property in 1866 from Frederick Ezekiel Edmonds for £540. They occupied the premises until 16th March 1887 when a sale was held at the Swan Hotel. Andrew D. Hatch bought the malting house for £455. The sale included:

'A 20 quarter malthouse (Quarter = 1 measure of capacity of grain -
1 qtr = 8 bushels) with kilns adjoining. Lately occupied by Messrs.
G. & T. Spencer, but now void. The malthouse has 4 floors, each 77
ft by 25 ft 6 ins, and in good repair.'[10]

It is uncertain when the malthouse stopped production. It was subsequently
used as storage premises by varying occupants. Finally the Bradford and
Melksham Rural District Council, who owned the property in September
1958, decided the building was unsafe and decided to accept the tender
from F. M. Feasey of Bath for £1,050 to demolish it. This was completed by
December 1958.

Church Street Malthouse, pictured in 1958. Abbey House is to the right

Malthouse, Frome Road

In 1808 W.G. Burcomb was in occupation of a house, orchard and land at Clay Farm, at 'Great Trowle'.[10] Great Trowle was an area that seems to have included a large swathe of land from Trowle Common to Frome Road. It is quite possible that the house was later used as the Barge Inn, Frome Road. By 1822 Edward Burcombe was landlord of the Barge Inn and Walter Burcombe was malting at the premises adjacent to the Inn.[12]

This malthouse in Frome Road was owned by the brewers G. & T. Spencer in 1841. It was situated on land now occupied by the housing development called The Maltings. By 1927 it was in the hands of Messrs E. Baily of Frome.[12] Unfortunately the malthouse was destroyed by fire on 14th March 1944. Following the fire, planning permission was granted by Bradford Urban District Council in December 1944 for a new roof on the building. During the early part of World War Two it was also used as an air raid shelter for the residents of the Frome Road area. Before the war large quantities of malt were despatched from the Baily's malthouse at Bradford Railway station

Other Maltsters and Brewers

Richard and John Bethal owned a malthouse in 1841. It was situated on the south-west side of Trowbridge Road at Poulton, and was run by Richard Blackmore.[8]

In addition to the foregoing information, some inns and public houses also malted and brewed their own ale. Some of those were: In 1841 James Crisp at the Queens Head in St Margaret's Street (later The Three Gables), who was listed as a maltster as well as publican.[8] By 1848 James had died and his wife Elizabeth Crisp was similarly described.[12]

At the top end of the town at the Rising Sun, Winsley Road, the inn features in an indenture of 1880 which refers to the brewery and cellars on the premises. During the sales of the Castle Hotel in July 1848 and later, in October 1895, both sale particulars included a large brewery, malt and hop rooms at the rear.[13]

An insurance policy dated 1st January 1877, shows the New Inn, Widbrook (later known as the Beehive Inn, Trowbridge Road). This policy covered the public house and brewery.[10]

The Bell Inn, Newtown was referred to in a valuation account in April 1897. The inventory mentions, amongst other items 'the brewery plant'. When the Lamb Inn, Bridge Foot was sold in 1914 the sale details included the brewhouse.

Bradford on Avon's Pubs

Note: The names of former pubs are given in grey lettering

Angel Inn - *see* New Bear Inn

Barge Inn 17 Frome Road

In 1808 W.G. Burcombe was in occupation of a house and land at Clay Farm, at 'Great Trowle', which included the Frome Road area. It was this house which was later used as the Barge Inn. This was around the time when the Kennet and Avon Canal opened. By 1822 Edward Burcombe was landlord of the inn and Walter Burcombe was malting at the premises adjacent to the inn.

By 1841 William Sainsbury was in the Barge which also included a Brewery and Malthouse. May 1914 the Barge was sold by Spencer's Brewery to Usher's Brewery of Trowbridge.

A wedding group posing for the camera in the garden in 1901; could this be the Sainsbury family?

48

A local innkeeper recently found long-forgotten papers revealing that the landlord of the Barge Inn in Bradford escorted 'Ladies of the Town' to the Carpenters Arms in order to warm the spirits of the boatmen!

In addition to Burcombe and Sainsbury, Thos. Dowling, M. Hiscocks (also a blacksmith), W.H. Grist, Leslie Masters, Alex Boswell (from 1939) and Dick Eades were all landlords of the premises.

Boswell was followed by Vic Woodley (1950) who had been Chelsea and England football goalkeeper and had won 19 caps for his country. He proudly displayed his caps in a glass cabinet behind the bar at the pub. Vic was also an excellent cricketer and I had the pleasure of playing with him before his retirement. An excellent skittle alley was added at the side of the Pub in the 1960s but was later demolished to make way for extra car parking.

The inn was made a Grade Two listed building by English Heritage in August 1974.

The present landlady, Jill Maytom-Jones, has been in charge since 1993 and more recently undertook the complete refurbishment of her extensive premises which includes a large garden and an attractive area overlooking the Kennet and Avon Canal. The Barge Inn is currently described as a rustic gastro pub with open fires, beer garden and restaurant facilities

Beef & Barge

Facing the Trowbridge Road on the southern outskirts of Braford on Avon, this pub is also adjacent to the Bradford on Avon Marina which opened in about 1990 and was originally christened The Gongoozler, an unusual pub name. Gongoozler means 'onlooker', in particular those who enjoy viewing the activity on canals. Following a change of ownership, the name became The Mill House, then the Beef & Barge. At the time of writing the freehold of the Beef & Barge is up for sale by owners Admiral Taverns.

The Beef & Barge 'Waterside Pub and Restaurant', with its TESCO-style clock turret.

Beehive formerly New Inn, 263 Trowbridge Road

The Register of Electors for 1833/5 shows Benjamin Matthews as occupier of the New Inn on land at the Folly, Widbrook.

A document of 1862 to the Overseers of the Poor and Constables of the Parish of Bradford, reveals that Robert Raymond applied for a licence 'to sell liquors by retail to be drunk or consumed in the house situate at Widbrook, known by the sign of the New Inn, in which I intend to keep as an Inn, Alehouse and victualling house'. Later, in 1877-82, an insurance policy of £500 was taken out by Elizabeth May to cover the New Inn and Brewery.[1]

From this time various Innkeepers occupied the New Inn: Frank Green, William Flay, Geo. Heritage, G.H. Grist. It was F.J. Hannay, who appears to have been *in situ* when the inn's sign was changed to The Beehive around 1915; this is when the inn was sold by Spencer's Brewery to Usher's Brewery.[2] Hannay was followed by G.J. Hunt, Alfred Hancock and Fred J. Parfitt (Fred's pontoon coach outings were legendary in the 1960s).

Other landlords followed, including Clive and Chris Crocker, formerly at the Bunch of Grapes in Silver Street. In 2005 Mark and Belinda House moved into the Beehive. The couple came to Bradford from Tunbridge Wells and, although a dairy farmer by trade, Mark had ten years' experience in managing pubs: 'It's been a long-term plan of ours. We've put all our pennies into this and we have a 19-year lease on the place, so we will be here for a while.' However by mid-2008 they had to sell the inn due to Mrs House's arthritis. When Punch Taverns took over they charged £37,000 a year rent. Sadly the Beehive closed in September 2008.[3]

Bell Inn Newtown

This inn, now No. 62 Newtown, was situated at the bottom of Conigre Hill where it meets Newtown. It bears a datestone of 1695 and the bracket from which a large bell hung can still be seen on the front of the house. Records show that the bell was transferred to the Bell pub at Potterne when Bradford's Bell Inn closed in 1965.[4]

The first authenticated record of the building as the Bell Inn was in 1766 when William Davis was assessed for rates on his stock. By 1773 Davis, who owned the property, employed William Cooper as tenant and by 1774 Widow Cooper was in occupation. A Church Rate book of 1730 indicates that Thomas Sumsion was the owner, he was a Maltster, so it is quite possible that beer was sold on the premises before 1766.

There are a few vague references, from various sources, which indicate the many tenants and owners who followed, including, in no particular order: Edward Selfe, Mrs Parsons, the Baker family, John Dory, John Bush, Frederick Woodman. Also Thomas Webb who was listed as Brewer and licensee; then George Bevan, William and Edwin Dew, Mrs Ann Stokes, William Selfe, Alfred George Selby, William Elliott, Mrs Jane Ann Elliott, Henry and Eliz. Stevens, Wm. and Charles Sturrock, E.T. Bannister, D.R. Davies and June and Jack Hamlyn. In some cases the above were not listed separately, and therefore may be either tenants or owners of The Bell.

The Bell Inn, Newtown, pictured in 1942

Another interesting landlord of The Bell was Flight-Lieutenant Jeremy (Jack) Fallows, who was Captain of Lancashire Cricket Club for the 1946 season.

I recall, as a young man, visiting the pub one summer's evening when the Lancashire cricket team visited. They were playing a match against Somerset at Bath. My autograph book gained many signatures during the evening. I understand Jack, his wife and his Bentley car moved to the Hungerford Arms at Farleigh Hungerford before retiring to Jersey. I believe that he served on the Lancashire Committee until 1971. He died at Macclesfield, on 20th January, 1974, aged 66.

Returning to the inn's earlier years: Bertram Niblett in his book *Memories of Bradford on Avon*, states that there was a small brewery beside the hill up to Middle Rank and Tory at the rear of Bell House, Newtown. To confirm this, James Baker was owner of The Bell until his death in 1832. In his will dated December 1822, he left the Bell Inn 'with Brewhouse, Stable building and premises etc.' to his son John Shoare Baker 'now in his occupation'.

Occupants of the Bell probably continued to brew their own beer until 1897, when Wilkins Brothers (the Brewers further along Newtown) bought the Inn from William Selfe. Prior to the sale, T. Lavington, Auctioneers of Devizes, included the Brewing Plant in their valuation. The Wilkins Brothers would of course have supplied the beer from their own expanding business.

It is interesting to note that, as in many other inns over the years, some of the publicans at the Bell had an additional occupation. Alfred George Selby is shown as being a hairdresser as well as innkeeper from 1898 to 1901. Also, Edwin Dew (aged 20 in 1881) was listed as Engine Driver and Licensed Victualler, with his two sisters, Ellen aged 21 and Marion aged 18, shown as Licensed Victuallers' Assistants. William Selfe was also a builder in the Frome Road area, in addition to his innkeeping.

The inn appeared to have prospered under the Wilkins Brothers' ownership until 1919 when their business floundered. In February 1920 the inn and premises were sold to Ushers Brewery of Trowbridge. The sale included 'cottage adjoining and site of three cottages at rear'.[4]

Approximately one year after Ushers bought the Inn, a curious incident was reported in the *Wiltshire Times* of February 1921. A man, George Wheeler, was summoned before Bradford Magistrates for leaving a horse and cart 'uncontrolled' on 3rd February 1921 outside the Bell Inn, Newtown. P.C. Stanley had observed the vehicle from 12.04 to 12.24 p.m. Wheeler, when emerging from the inn said he'd only been in for the ashbin! His employer Mr Doel pleaded on Wheeler's behalf, but to no avail. The magistrates fined him 10 shillings (50p).

During December 1951, in an effort to boost trade, Ushers constructed a small skittle alley at the Bell. This was one of the venues for the Bradford Summer Skittles League, in which I played for a local team. The alley was very short in length and the floor was covered in linoleum, which was quite an uneven surface. I had the reputation of bowling a very fast ball. The evening in question was hot and balmy and the small window at the end of the alley was wide open. I bowled one particular ball, which hit a bump on the alley, lifted into the air on to the top of the front pin. It shot up even higher on to the top of a piano which was positioned just below the window. The ball careered out of the window, down the lower part of Conigre Hill, on down Newtown, then into Market Street. Later a team-mate chased after it and recovered it in front of the Swan Hotel!

In addition to skittles, darts and cribbage were encouraged at the Bell. Unfortunately trade decreased and during a board meeting in January 1965, Ushers Directors agreed that in view of loss of trade the Bell Inn be closed and it be sold with a reserve price of £2,000. The Inn closed on 6th April 1965. Ushers eventually sold the delicensed house to Malcolm Macleod for £2,500 on 31st March 1966.[2]

Brewhouse – see New Bear Inn

Bunch of Grapes Silver Street

Thomas Halse occupied this 18th century building in 1822 as the Bunch of Grapes and in 1823-7 William Harris.[5] By the mid to late 19th century the Chemists Thomas and Emanuel Taylor occupied the building, and gradually turned over to become wine merchants and gave up the Chemist side of the business in approx. 1880. They then opened a shop and warehouse on the opposite side of the road.

The Taylors were there in both premises until the 1930s. Further landlords followed including, amongst others, Herbert Burgess, A.S. Barrett and W. Weeks and Brian Cater.

English Heritage gave the building Grade Two listing in 1974.

The Grapes was refurbished in recent years, and while other pubs in the area have chosen to modernize the traditional look, the Grapes decided to retain its old world charm. They also provide restaurant facilities specializing in tasty pies.

Canal Tavern 49 Frome Road

This Inn is constructed of local freestone and backs onto the Kennet and Avon canal, immediately below Bradford lock. The origins of the pub are rooted firmly in the waterway with the earliest licences given to the Edmonds family.[5] This is confirmed by the 1851 and '61 censuses showing Robert Edmonds as occupier and as boat builder and beer retailer. By 1871 Robert is listed solely as Innkeeper, Canal Tavern. The 1881 census gives his wife Elizabeth as Innkeeper, Robert having died in 1876.

The Canal Tavern, pictured in 1915, before the entrance porch was added. (Photo courtesy of current landlord, Mark Randall)

At the tavern were stables for housing horses used in connection with the canal traffic.[6] During WW1 the narrow boat *Bittern* was purchased by the Red Cross, for use as a hospital boat to convey wounded soldiers to Avoncliff. The horse that drew the barge was stabled at the Canal Tavern and the barge was moored at the wharf nearby.

The tavern was sold in 1885 to Wadsworth Brewery, Devizes for £402 with fixtures £63.[7] Following the Edmonds family, other landlords occupied the house; amongst others were Thomas Thomson, Jacob Bailey, Jasper Lewis, John Adye, William Henry Groves and J. Timbrell.

The book, *Haunted Wiltshire* published in 2009 indicates that 'a shadow was seen from outside the Canal Tavern, crossing the living room window by a previous landlady and landlord plus shadows were seen in the utility room. In the area of the bar, the sound of church music has been heard and a possible active area for poltergeist activities was experienced in the area of the stairs.

In recent years a restaurant has been included in the pub's facilities and live music is another attraction. 1988 saw a group of boaters form a club using the inn as its H.Q.; their motto is 'panic slowly'.

Castle Inn (Hotel) 10 Mount Pleasant

The Castle was, originally a square Georgian house of ashlar under a pyramidal slate covered roof. It has a stone porch on Tuscan-style columns on the garden front. A single-storey pub front was added on the front side.[8]

A fine lamp and handsome porch herald the entrance to the Castle from its pleasant garden which affords views across Bradford on Avon towards Salisbury Plain

The inn , at the top of Mason's Lane appears, in 1841, to have been no more than the house of George Newman, a beer retailer. It was not until 1848 that reference is made to the Castle Inn with Newman as publican.[9]

Many landlords followed Newman, including, Alfred Blackmore, Austin Rossiter, Henry J. Blackmore, William Moody, James Godden, F.C.Banks and Eddy Young. The Castle, Brewery and Stables were, in July 1875, sold to Joseph Sparks of Bradford for £320.[10]

Latterly owned by the Lounge Group, in 2007 the pub was remodelled and sympathetically restored to a high standard including excellent restaurant facilities.

Carpenters Arms Inn – see Ship Inn

Cross Keys Frome Road

The Cross Keys Inn was situated in Frome Road approximately where Keates Garage once stood, now Barton Close housing.[11]

An early reference to the inn was in 1808 when William Dyke was in residence. From 1822 Joseph Buxton was the landlord. He obviously fell foul of the courts, as in 1825 Buxton (who was described as a Victualler) was brought before Thomas Tugwell and Thomas Hosier Sanders for an offence against his Alehouse recognizance. This is a bond entered into when applying for a licence. He forfeited £5, this being his first offence, with 25/= costs. Again in 1827 he was brought before the same magistrates for a further unspecified offence. Again he forfeited a further £5, being his second offence, this time with 20/= costs.[12] Despite these misdemeanours Joseph Buxton was still landlord in 1831.

By 1841 Richard Pearce a Methodist, who also owned the Maidenhead Inn in Pippet Street, owned the Cross Keys with James Martin as landlord. Under Pearce's direction sobriety reigned at the inn and it was said that customers were only allowed one pint of beer at each visit.

Writing in 1873 the Rev. Christophers recalled that there once was a small room behind the bar, used for Methodist meetings.[13]

The inn was demolished when the Great Western Railway established the railroad through the town in the 1850s.[12]

Crown Inn Woolley

The Crown Inn, Woolley was situated in a house, which is No. 2 Crown Court, Woolley.[14]

In 1838 John Kittelty occupied the house and was described in Robson's Directory of that year as a Beer Retailer. By 1841 he was a grocer as well as Beer Retailer on this Crown Court site. In addition to his wife Grace, the house was inhabited by his daughter Amelia, three grandchildren and two servants.[15] It was not until 1848 that the house was commonly known as the Crown Inn.[16]

Further landlords followed, with William Austin in 1871 (with Thomas Ball Silcox as owner) and John King in 1878. By 1881 King had died and his Widow Elizabeth King was listed as Cloth Mender in addition to Publican.[18] The Town Land Tax Returns of 1883-4, lists Mrs King as owner, but one year later the building was listed in the Woolley Grange Estate's papers.

There does not appear to be any reference to the Crown Inn after this date.

Dandy Lion 35 Market Street

In the late 18th and early 19th centuries this premises was the grocery shop of the Smart family; Thomas Smart's name board is still underneath the present one. Another grocer succeeded him, and Nichols and Bushell's business continued until the mid-1960s. In the 1970s it was converted into a restaurant called the Shandon Steak House with Mr Power as manager. In the 1980s under new ownership it became the Ancient Fowl and shortly after became the Dandy Lion, as it is today.

The Dog & Fox 33 Ashley Road

The 1841 census shows Hester Tucker as victualler, aged 50; she occupied one of the cottages which later became the Dog and Fox. It is built of rubble stone and has some 17th century features.[17] By 1871 it had become the Dog & Fox with John Tucker as landlord.[18]

The pub was sold to Spencer's Brewery in March 1892 for £480 and then to Usher's brewery in 1914.

Various innkeepers followed Tucker, including , Mrs John Tucker, Mrs M.A. Gerrish, Jasper Lewis, Albert Henry Gerrish and Mrs Gerrish. In 1952 Mr E.C. Gater became the licensee, the family continued in the pub and Alan Bishop, son-in-law to Mr Gater took over the tenancy in 1990, Alan's son, Adam taking over until the lease ran out in 2011. The pub was in the hands of the same family for almost 60 years.

The Dog & Fox

In the summer of 2011 a new management team Andy and Jo, came to the pub and completed renovations. A local resident stated that it is a traditionally run family pub, you won't find any fruit machines or juke box, simply a warm welcome with reasonably priced home cooked meals, real ales and cask ciders. A hidden gem in Bradford on Avon.

Fisherman Inn St Margarets Hill

The Fisherman Inn is referred to by the late local historian Bertram Niblett as 'one of a group of cottages known as The Square, in St Margarets Hill.' A number of garages now stand on this site at the top of St Margarets Steps.

A rate assessment of 1808 shows that James Mead was the landlord at the time. No further reference can be found on this Inn.

French Horn

The French Horn Inn was situated by the entrance to station approach, next to what is now the Grocery Basket shop, in a small parking area presently owned by Mr Burbidge. The rate assessments of 1808-10 indicate that Joseph Provis was the landlord of the Inn at the time. It was one of a small group of old cottages which were demolished in March 1935.

George Inn 47 Woolley Street

This Inn perhaps stands on the site of the New Inn, which in 1714 existed in Tooley St (Woolley Street) and leased in 1734 by the Duke of Kingston to Mary Whatley.[20] In 1841 the block was of three houses one of which was a factory another a beer house, all appear to be of different dates.[21]

Henry Green was the landlord in 1878 followed by T.G. Hillier in 1886 and then by Emma Hillier who was mine host until 1935.

A local resident, Mrs Elsie Wilkins, recalls that during WW2 expectant mothers came down from London when approximately eight months pregnant. They stayed at the Grange, Woolley before having their child at Bradford Maternity Hospital, Berryfield. At times they walked along Woolley Street to the George for a drink. The mainly male customers who were not used to seeing females in the bar, especially pregnant ones, frowned upon this!

For many years the George has been the HQ and main hub of the Woolley Music Festival, gaining a worldwide reputation. In addition to this there are often live bands during the week and at weekends, which draw in good crowds.

Green Dragon

An alehouse called the Green Dragon was situated on the site of what is now the Scribbling Horse Café (34, Silver Street). A land tax assessment of 1773-4 indicates that the landlady was Widow Baylie. From 1784 until 1801 the landlord was Samuel White. Later tenants were John Smith (1813), William Harding (1815-20), James Mead (1823), James Crisp (1834), later James Howell, then James Comely (1841) and William Dix. From 1801 to 1809 Thomas Spender was the landlord at the Inn, which was at the time described as being in Horse Street.

Greyhound

This inn stood in St Margaret's Hill, then known as Morgans Hill. It was a coaching inn. The stables and coach house, Morgans Lodge, next to St Margaret's Court,[22] is used as a private dwelling and was formerly the home of Harold Fassnidge, author of the standard history of the town *Bradford on Avon: Past & Present*.

Morgans Lodge,
St Margaret's Hill,
once the Greyhound pub

The Inn Huntingdon Street

Two cottages, Nos 3 and 4 Huntingdon Street just opposite the Chapel, were once an inn. In a rate book of 1834/5 John Tucker is listed as a Victualler in that area; it is quite possible he was a landlord of this inn.

Mrs Turtell, an long-time resident of Huntingdon Street, recalls that one of the houses still has the brewers delivery hatch, where barrels of beer were lowered into the cellars below.

King's Arms Coppice Hill - see King's Arms and Brewery, pages 40-43

King's Head Whitehill

Formerly situated in Whitehill, the old King's Head Inn is a private dwelling, now 13 Whitehill. It was numbered No. 16 prior to the late 1960s.[23]

The former King's Head, Whitehill

An early record indicates that Richard Hayward was landlord there from 1808 to 1810.[24] By 1822 Francis Jenkins was mine host until 1850, when a number of landlords occupied the Inn, including: Francis Higgins, Simeon Sylvester, George Sidnell, John Gifford, William & Elizabeth Barley, Frank Collett, Frank Mattock, E. Southwood, Charles Bryant, Mr & Mrs J. Matthews, G.F. Long, Thomas Carter, Wm. Bailey, Morris Dyer and Wm. J. Butcher.

In 1931 John Bigwood was appointed landlord. This started a long period when the Bigwood family were tenants of the house. By 1939 John's wife Ethel Bigwood was in charge, until her retirement in September 1946. In a testament to her, Usher's Brewery, who had bought the property from Wilkins Bros. in 1920, wrote in their in house magazine:

'Mrs Bigwood held the distinction of being one of the few women licensees of Ushers. Although dealing with the manifold difficulties of the war years in a masterly manner, she has long looked forward to retiring from the business and we feel sure she deserves a rest. Her nephew and his wife, Mr & Mrs Jack Bigwood have taken over the King's Head. Mr Bigwood has been a rubber worker in the town for 20 Years and we feel sure his many friends in the town will stand him in good stead in his new sphere as a landlord.'

By 1958 C.H. Dacre-Tyler was the landlord and in 1961 the pub was obviously not doing well. During an Executive Meeting in October 1961 Ushers' directors were informed that the takings at the King's Head were only £30 per week which was proving unprofitable. It was agreed that the pub be closed. This happened on 16th October 1961.[25] It was in February 1963 that Usher's de-licensed the house and sold the property to Robert James Horlick for £1,600.

King's Head Woolley

An early mention of this hostelry was in 1774 when Thomas Johnson, a J.P. for Wiltshire and a clothier, inherited from his brother James, 'a public house called the Kings Head in Woolley'. Later an indenture of 1791 refers to two cottages at Woolley. The agreement between a Mrs Johnson and Mrs T. Coombs states that 'the messuages, cottages, or tenements, with stable, garden and appurtenances there unto adjoining and now converted into a Public House and called or known by the sign, Kings Head.'

During 1800, William Coombs, a relative of the above Mrs Coombs made a will also referring to the above premises and being used as an inn, called the Kings Head 'now in occupation of myself and tenants'. The will was proved in 1816.[27]

A rate assessment of 1808 gives details of Wm. Coombs of Woolley in the house, with stock also being taken into consideration. It is thought that the house was in what is now the Woolley Green area of the town.

Lamb Inn see Scribbling Horse Inn

Maidenhead Inn Pippett Street (now Market Street)

The first mention of the property situated at no. 29 Market Street, who owned other proerty in the town, and now occupied by the Bradford on Avon Club, was in 1611 when an agreement refers to 'these premises, comprising two small buildings with gardens and malthouse'. It is here that the Maidenhead Inn came into being, together with stables, well and courtyard which were used by wayfarers for many years.

By 1738 Daniel Bright sold the premises to David Lea, the inn then described as 'all that messuage or tenement commonly called the Maidenhead and situate in Pippett Street, together with malthouse, stables and several buildings.' Lea sold the property to Wm. Abraham and Wm. James in 1749. Their ownership was fairly short, for in 1755, Richard Pearce bought the Maidenhead, when modifications to the premises took place, which included a newly erected building to replace the malthouse. This new building was the Methodist Chapel. A new frontage to the inn was constructed at the time.

By 1766, Richard and Betty Pearce, the innholders, sold the property to Wm. Wilshire and Edward Pearce and, like Richard Pearce, these two were also Methodists.

Bradford on Avon Town Club, formerly the Maidenhead Inn

The property changed hands many times during the ensuing years, with many occupants to the tenements and inn. Later Joseph Rawlings, the Printer and Engraver, used the inn area, with the Post Office next door, in Pippett Street, as Market Street was then known. The Bradford Conservative Club were using the property in 1903, John Moulton being the owner. Following Moulton's death in 1925, the property was auctioned later that year, and purchased for the purpose of establishing a social club known as the Bradford on Avon Club, as it remains today.[27]

The last reference to the property as the Maidenhead Inn appears to be in the Land Tax Assessments of 1780.

Market Tavern Church Street/Market Street

The Market Tavern was one of a number of small houses situated at the junction of Church Street and Market Street (formerly Pippett Street). The houses had gabled roofs and diamond-paned windows and showed evidence of being timber framed.[28] A woodcut by Alfred Spragg of about 1840 indicates that an inside chimney carried the date 1636, a gable showed a date of 1687. A sign on the outside of the building appears to reveal that it was then called the New Market Tavern.

The block of houses were demolished to make way for the Town Hall in 1854/5 and around a hundred years later in 1954 it became the Catholic Church.

Rawlings, writing in 1887, gives an interesting insight into the site:

Market Tavern by the Bristolian and topographical artist William Walter Wheatley (1811-1885) who lived in both Bath and Rode

'The modern residents of Bradford have probably almost forgotten the quaintly antique appearance of the old Flemish looking houses which stood in the Market Place in bye-gone times; they were demolished some years since, the site being appropriated to the splendid edifice erected thereon by the Bradford Town Hall and Market Company. These old houses were by many supposed to have been built at the time of an arrival of some Flemish weavers, who were probably induced to live here when the weaving and making of the woollen cloths became the principal trade of the town, possibly by the ancestors of the Methuen family.'

Unfortunately no mention of the Market Tavern was made by Rawlings.

Specific details of owners and occupiers are uncertain but it is interesting to note that from a street directory of 1793, Edward White is listed as a Victualler in the Wine Tavern.

White certainly lived in the Church Street area and it is quite possible that he occupied the Market Tavern premises. By 1838-48 Israel Fielding was listed as a Beer Retailer in Church Street,[29] but in Slaters Directory of 1852 he is shown as occupier of the New Market. This together with other records indicate that this was the same Inn.[30]

Masons Arms 52 Newtown

The Masons Arms dates from the late 17th to early 18th century. It was originally built as a house and later converted into the inn. The Land Tax assessment of 1773-80 gives the Innkeeper as Jn Egerton. Pigot's Directory lists the Masons Arms tenanted by William Deson (or Denson) in 1822 and in 1830 by his widow Phyllis. In 1842 Elizabeth Silk is given as tenant.

The 1891 Census recorded that Frederick Rossiter was brewing at the Masons Arms, Newtown, as well as being the publican. An 1894 advertisement, still mentions Rossiter as 'Landlord of the Mason's Arms and Brewery, Newtown', and went on to state that 'as he had increased his facilities he was able to supply Home-brewed Beers and Ales. The product of best Malt and Hops in casks of any size – Prices at 10d., 1s., 1s.2d., 1s 4d., 1s.6d., per gallon.'

The 7th June 1902 issue of the *Wiltshire Times* reported that the Masons Arms Inn, along with its brewery, was to be auctioned at the Swan Hotel that week. Mr Harrold, the auctioneer, said it was a house admirably suited to the purposes of an Inn. It was situated in an essentially beer drinking district, the present trade was about 14 barrels a week, the takings last year amounted to £2,000. The auction of the property started at £1,000 and went to £3,000, then by bids of £100 to £4,200, at which figure it was sold to the Oakhill Brewery Company. It was at this time that brewing on the premises ceased.

The inn continued to thrive throughout the two world wars and beyond. In 2004 the police received numerous complaints from members of the public and in early March 2004 a report appeared in the *Evening Advertiser* as follows:

'A pub landlord has blasted police for using over the top tactics during a raid on his premises. Dave Simmons who runs the

Masons Arms in Bradford-on-Avon, said officers acted as if they were hunting for the Kray twins or Jamaican gangsters when they raided his pub. A team of officers from Melksham and Bradford were tasked with rooting out under aged drinkers after a series of complaints from the public. Three 17 year-old youths were found drinking alcohol on the premises. One was arrested and bailed on suspicion of possessing cannabis with intent to supply. A forged ID card was also seized.

Mr Simmons said two vanloads of officers arrived at the pub just before 9.30 p.m. and 15 officers jumped out. They were totally out of order in the way they spoke to everybody. They shouted at everyone to stop, including the staff. Customers who wanted to go to the toilets were followed. They took everyone's particulars asking names and ages. We are very vigilant and do not serve under age people, we ask everyone for ID. I want to know exactly what we have done wrong.'

Police said they had received a series of complaints about the running of the Masons Arms over the past few weeks, mainly focusing on underage drinking.

Shortly after, in 2005 the Masons Arms was closed and sold to Amek Investments (Commercial) Ltd. for development into two dwellings.

Mason's Arms Inn & Brewery,
NEWTOWN, BRADFORD-ON-AVON.

F. ROSSITER,
Having increased facilities is now able to supply

HOME-BREWED BEER & ALES
The product of Best Malt & Hops in Casks of any size.

PRICES—10d., 1/-, 1/2, 1/4 and 1/6 per Gallon.

Wines and Spirits
OF THE FINEST QUALITY ON DRAUGHT OR IN BOTTLE.
ORDERS BY POST PROMPTLY ATTENDED TO.

New Bear Inn/Hotel previously The Brewhouse and Angel Inn

This inn was situated in Silver Street, in the house now named Silver Street House.

An early indenture of 1731 refers to the property as the Brewhouse and later as the Angel. By 1736 its name had again changed to The New Bear.

The 1731 lease, for one year, details the transfer to Samuel Baber, Innholder, from John Cooper of Trowbridge. The rate books of the period show a seven-fold increase in the rateable value, which indicates a huge change to the building and perhaps the time when it became a Hotel and the New Bear.[31] In 1790 Thomas Johnson of Woolley House left the freehold of the NewBear to his wife Ann in his will.

In the nineteenth century, the New Bear and the Swan were always referred to as the two main inns in the town. Below is an advertisement from the *Bath & Cheltenham Gazette* of 1815 shows one Benjamin Mason describing himself as the new landlord of the New Bear Inn:

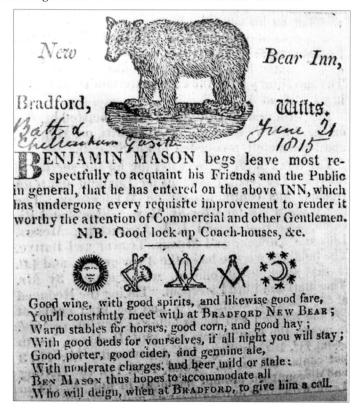

New Bear Inn, Bradford, Wilts.
Bath & Cheltenham Gazette — June 21 1815

BENJAMIN MASON begs leave most respectfully to acquaint his Friends and the Public in general, that he has entered on the above INN, which has undergone every requisite improvement to render it worthy the attention of Commercial and other Gentlemen.
N.B. Good lock-up Coach-houses, &c.

Good wine, with good spirits, and likewise good fare,
You'll constantly meet with at BRADFORD NEW BEAR;
Warm stables for horses, good corn, and good hay;
With good beds for yourselves, if all night you will stay;
Good porter, good cider, and genuine ale,
With moderate charges, and beer mild or stale:
BEN MASON thus hopes to accommodate all
Who will deign, when at BRADFORD, to give him a call.

By 1832 John Spencer, the brewer in Whiteheads Lane, owned the inn; following the demise of the Spencer's brewery, the inn was sold in 1914 to Usher's Brewery of Trowbridge.[33] Records show that it became the town's leading hotel second only to the Swan in Church Street.[32]

From the mid-18th century the New Bear was used by the Justices of the Peace for their Petty Sessions. As mentioned earlier, one James Elliott was brought before Bradford's Justice of the Peace in 1794 at the New Bear for illegally selling cider.

The New Road Act of 1841 brought a committee, including the Justices of the Peace for Wiltshire and Somerset, to the town. Their first meeting was at the New Bear when they passed the act to turnpike the road from Bradford to Wingfield.[34]

An advert in a directory of 1911 refers to the Inn as follows:

'New Bear, Family and Commercial Hotel, G.H. Woodstock, Proprietor; Luncheons, Dinners and Teas at any time for large or small parties; Moderate tariff, in Silver Street.'[34]

It is interesting to note that on the 1st April 1834, Lord Methuen's records show that:

'a petition was received from the Hundred Jury of Court Leet at the Court Baron of P Methuen Esq, Lord of The Manor of Bradford, held at the New Bear Inn. Subject: The Ancient Market House and Town Hall, pulled down owing to its ruinous state. The Jurors and Inhabitants state there is no proper place to meet. They request a Market Place and Town Hall be erected for public business by Mr P. Methuen or grant tolls of the market at a nominal rent.'[35]

No information is given as to the result of this petition, but we do know of course that the New Town Hall in Church Street/Market Street, was opened in 1855, on the site of the old Market Tavern Inn.

The Hotel was also used for Property Auctions, an example being in December 1847 when houses in Wine Street, Morgans Hill (St Margarets Hill) and Bridge Street were sold by auction.

In one of their booklets, published in 1950, Ushers the Brewers, and still owners of the hotel at the time wrote:

'The New Bear graces the street with regency style architecture and in spite of its name is quite an interesting old house, dating back to the 18th century and retaining some unusual features. Antiquarians will find the panelling and cupboards in the bar particularly interesting. The cupboards are shell-shaped at the top. The fluted pillars to the fireplace and the original dent-de-lion cornice are also worthy of notice.'[36]

At that time the New Bear had a catering licence for snacks and B & B.[36]

Over the years the Inn/Hotel changed hands on numerous occasions, some of those being W. White, John Rogers, John Deverell, J. Wiltshire, Benj. & Elizabeth Mason, Samuel & Ann Mundy, Jacob Gingell, Wm. Tucker Feltham, Herbert Hole, John & Jemima Harman, G. Woodstock, Mrs Amy Ascott, and Grantly Thomas.[37] In 1930, Wilfred George May was appointed manager and he remained there until 1948. Mr & Mrs S.A.J. Boxwell as managers then made it their home. It was in 1952 that Sid Boxwell, while preparing a bedroom for decoration, discovered the following carved in the panelling of the bedroom window: 'W. Syms, August 27th 1794.'[33]

Due to economic circumstances Ushers Brewery were unable to keep the New Bear open and had, by 1958, closed its doors for business. After this date the building deteriorated and the *Wiltshire Times* stated that it had been 'falling into the street for years.' Fortunately the Bradford on Avon Preservation Trust purchased the house in 1975. Renovation work was put in hand in 1977 and it was opened by the Duke of Grafton in 1978. The run-down listed house was sympathetically converted into flats which retained many of the original Georgian features.[37]

New Inn, Bath Road

This 18th century coaching Inn is now No. 198 Bath Road and named Clifton House. However, in 1720 the house was occupied by Robert Hanny, victualler, and so was probably an alehouse. The construction of a new road in the 1780/90s (now Bath Road) led to the establishment of this inn, in order to serve the additional customers who passed along the road.[38] The 1785 Land Tax indicates George Kittlety was using part of the premises and the front by the road probably became the New Inn at this time. In 1810 Kittlety still occupied the front range and Wm Coombs lived in the range to the rear (see King's Head, Woolley). In 1834-7 Benjamin Matthew leased the inn, then moved to the Lamb Inn.

An early reference to the inn was in 1822 when John Rees Jones was granted a license to sell ale.[39] He remained at the inn until 1833 when Benjamin Matthews occupied the premises and by 1838 he had moved to the Lamb Inn in the centre of the town. George Newman became the new owner and employed Joseph Clarke as publican.[40] Pigot's 1842 Directory gives the innkeeper as Joseph Clarke. In about 1851 Wm. Merrick, solicitor, bought the property and the name was transferred to premises across the road, opposite the present road into the Berryfield estate. By 1865 William Bainton was custodian and was described as Innkeeper and wool weaver in the 1861 census. Bainton was still an Innkeeper in 1871. The 1881 census does not indicate that it was an inn at that date.

An indenture between Charles Henry Wills of Winsley, a retired Grocer and Charles Herbert of Salisbury indicates that Wills bought the property in July 1898 for £600. The agreement went on to say:

> 'that messuage or tenement and shop with garden court and appurtenances to the same, situate in Bearfield, Bradford. Now in occupation of Edwin Slade, fronting the road leading from Bradford to Bath and adjoining a lane called Church Lane or Winsley Road, and also the shop and bakehouse now used by Edwin Slade. A!so all that messuage or tenement formerly called the New Inn and also all that small tenement approached by a flight of steps from the front of the New Inn aforesaid, all of which shops and messuages and premises are situate contiguous to each other and abut on the high road leading from Bradford to Bath.'

In a street directory of 1909 an advertisement appeared which stated: 'Edwin Slade & Son, Bakers, Grocers, and Provision Merchants – No 1 Bath Road, established upwards of 11 years.' This appears to confirm some of the details in the indenture.

Talking to Bertram Niblett some years ago, he recalled that when the inn was at the height of its popularity, the innkeeper would place a servant in the gazebo which is situated to the side of the house, nearer to the churchyard. The servant was required to look out for approaching coaches and travellers to entice them in, and then warn the inn and stable staff of the forthcoming customers. He carried on to say that the façade of the building was, as it is today, with the exception that the main doorway has been blocked in with a window at the centre. Beside it was the cellar entrance where barrels of ale were rolled down by the draymen.

Clifton House, formerly the New Inn. The cellar entrance is visible to the left.

Old Bear Inn 26 Silver Street

The Old Bear appears in the earliest Church Rate Book in 1726 as The Bear, before then it had been leased to William Grant followed by Richard Grant. In 1752 it was let to Mary and Ann Grant. A deed of 1767 describes it as the Old Bear, the property of the Duke of Kingston. The rate book of 1808 shows John Adams as Innkeeper and in 1830 Samuel Mundy as occupier.[1] William Stokes appears as Innkeeper and Brewer in 1855.[41,42]

The Inn was rebuilt in the 19th century as part of a road-widening scheme. In May 1914 Spencers Brewery sold the pub to Ushers Brewery, Trowbridge.[43]

Numerous landlords occupied the premises over the years including Mrs Rossiter, John Robert Lowries, Percy Cottle and Kerr Borland.

The Bear Inn, Silver Street, formerly the Old Bear Inn opposite the New Bear Inn (now Silver Street House)

In the early part of the 2000s the pub closed and re-opened in August 2010 after seven months of renovation by Blindmans Brewery of Frome, it is now a four bedroomed Inn with real ale, cider and good quality food.

Plough Inn Bradford Leigh

James Gerrish was listed only as beer retailer in 1838 at the 18th century premises in Bradford Leigh. By 1852 he was listed as innkeeper at the Plough Inn and continued as such until 1878 when Robert Mizen took over. In 1894 George Mould was in house until he died in 1909 when his wife Mary continued the tenancy.[44] Spencer's Brewery sold the pub to Ushers Brewery, Trowbridge in 1914. The sale details stated 'Inn with garden and outbuildings'.[45]

The pub was next to the Bradford Leigh Fair field. Just after the Second World War. I attended the fair on 24th August and popped into the pub, only to be faced with a grumpy landlord, who appeared to be very reluctant to serve anyone, I think the extra number of customers from the fair was a little to much for him!

Over the past forty years the pub has been refurbished and a wing added on in the 1980s.It is now a family-run establishment offering fine food, real ales and a warm, friendly atmosphere.

Plough Inn Trowbridge Road

This inn occupies what were originally two, three-storey houses on the end of a short early 19th century terrace called Regents Place.[46]

Charles Grist made an alehouse application in June 1834. He applied for a licence to sell beer at Regents Place, such house not having been kept or used as an Inn, Alehouse or Victualling house within the previous years.

By 1838 Job Wastfield was resident in the house as Beer Retailer. After Job died in 1846 his wife Ann and son Job Jnr. took over. Ann died in 1852 and Job Jnr succeeded her in 1855 he was listed as Innkeeper and Brewer in the Plough Inn.[47]

Past innkeepers include John Ricketts, Tom Orman, Edward Batchelor and Edward Francis; Francis Sprules took over in 1935. It was he who, during the Second World War, when having to go down to his cellar for more supplies, descended through the trap door which was just inside the side door to the pub. On returning from the cellar he would allow the trap door to slam down very loudly to frighten customers into thinking a bomb had dropped.

Others followed including A.F. Button and Bill Martin. The present landlord has a sign below his Plough Inn sign, on the Trowbridge Road stating 'No Food; Crap Beer; Bad Hospitality'.

Plume of Feathers, 9/10 St Margaret's Street

The two premises, 9/10 St Margarets Street, were for 77 years owned by the ironmonger family of Bryants. It was once the Plume of Feathers Inn. Clive and Sheila Bryant, who retired in March 2000, and the last of the family to occupy the building, believe the deeds show it was an inn in the 1700s.

A directory dated 1911 includes an advert which refers to the premises as follows: 'ART STUDIOS, (Proprietors H. & G. Morse, late F Shettle) Photographic Artists, Enlargers and Picture Framers, 9/10 St Margaret's

Street, Bradford.'

Noreen Cambourne (née Bryant) recalled that when her family took over the buildings from the photographers, they found hundreds of photographic plates in store there. They were thrown down an old well at the rear of the shop. The well was later filled in.

*Restaurant in St Margaret's Street,
once the Plume of Feathers*

Queen's Head, 2 St Margaret's Street

This coaching inn, situated at 2, St Margaret's Street, was actually the middle house of three 17th century houses, but now interconnected, and in recent years known as the Three Gables.[48] A family of Miles owned the Inn in the 18th century and the family head was a maltster and a baker. It is thought he built the house next to the Three Gables, now called the Georgian Lodge.[49] The Queen's Head was established in the early 18th century and, in 1793, occupied by John Atkins. Many owners and licensees followed, some of whom were James and Elizabeth Crisp (for at least part of their forty-plus years at the inn, Col. William Miles was the owner), John Groom, James Green, Edwin Crees, Joseph Sweetland, George Coombe Perry, Lewis Weaver, Thomas Weaver, Thomas Braxton, James Mitcham, George Shipway and Albert Chamberland.[50]

As a coaching inn, the Queen's Head was ideally situated in the centre of the town. In 1841, Hillier and May were running wagons from the Inn three times a week for Trowbridge and London. John Bazer left the Queen's Head for London every Monday and Friday and John Simons departed for Salisbury every Monday.[51]

It was in September 1892, that Mr G.C. Perry the owner of the Queen's Head instructed the auctioneers, Foley & Son & Mundy to sell the premises. The auction took place at the premises. In addition to the inn it included 260-gallon copper furnace and fixings, a 20-bushel oak mash tub, hop press and stand, malt mill, piping to river, lead pipe and piping to well and two fermenting vessels. The copper sign in front of house, together with other pieces of beer making equipment and household items, including three engravings by Hogarth.[52]

During the period that G. & T. Spencer's owned the Inn, the brewing side of the Queens Head business ceased, as of course Spencer's own brewery supplied the beer.

By 1911/12 business at the Queen's Head waned and at a brewster session in May 1912, Bradford's Licensing Authority considered the licence of the inn at 2 St Margaret's Street. It reviewed the poor trade in the past year. The inn was only 168 yards from the Three Horse Shoes, 186 yards from the Kings Arms and 183 from the front door of the Swan Hotel, and moreover there were several licensed houses in Silver Street. The Queen's Head was only reserved for further consideration in 1911 because the Lamb Inn was within 100 yards and it was then referred to the authority.

Following considerable deliberations they considered the Queen's Head should be closed, with John Henry Griffin as the last licensee.[53]

The Queen's Head, St Margaret's Street, now part of the Three Gables Restaurant

Following the closure of the Queen's Head, Spencer's Brewery leased all three of the properties, (Nos. 1, 2 and 3 St Margaret's Street) which they now owned. By July 1914 Spencer's Brewery and properties were bought by Usher's Brewery, of Trowbridge and Lot 6 of the sale included:

'Shop and premises being no 1 St Margaret's Street, now in the occupation of Mrs Matilda Barnett on a quarterly tenancy. Also no. 2 St Margaret's Street being the shop and premises adjoining, formerly the Queen's Head Inn, including cellars, brewing store room and dwelling house, but now used as a cycle shop by Mr Charles Perkins on a fortnightly tenancy. Also shop and premises adjoining being No. 3 St Margaret's Street, now in the occupation of Mr J. Mitchell on a weekly tenancy with a gross annual rental of £34.18s.0d.'[54]

It was shortly after this date that Spencer Moulton, the rubber manufacturers, whose factory was just across the bridge, used the buildings as their works canteen. It is uncertain how long the rubber company occupied the premises. A suggestion has been made that the Moulton family converted the three dwellings into one, as it is today, naming it the Three Gables. Eventually Spencer Moulton erected their own canteen building in the Lamb Yard.[55]

By 1933 the newly married Edie Bachelor and Bert Scrine moved in to run the premises as a restaurant. The Three Gables was managed by the couple for 28 years. Following her husband's death in 1958, Mrs Scrine ran the business until she died in 1961 aged 59 years. Her only child, Mrs Janet Davey took over the business.[56]

The Three Gables was a restaurant or café, with varying occupants until it was vacated in the late 1980s when it remained empty and unused for 23 years until eventually being completely refurbished and reopening as the Three Gables Restaurant in 2011.

Queen Victoria Bridge Foot

An early reference to the Queen Victoria was in 1841 when the inn was described as being at the Bridge Foot. This appears to be one of the number of houses, now amalgamated into no. 2 Silver Street and known as 'Out to Lunch'.[57] It was probably established as an Inn in order to honour the new Queen who came to the throne in 1837. At the time Charles Spackman was the owner and Joseph Fott was the Publican.

At that time the inn played its part in providing the town with coaching facilities. A two-horse coach called at the Queen Victoria daily. One left the Lopes Arms, Westbury and collected passengers for Bath at 9.30 a.m. and returned from the Greyhound, Bath to Bradford at 7.30 p.m. and on to Westbury.

All references to the Queen Victoria disappeared by 1848 when Joseph Fott was publican at the Old Bear Inn, Silver Street.

Red Lion 2 Church Street

This inn was at No. 2 Church Street in 1767 (then called Trinity Street).

It was owned by the Duke of Kingston who leased the premises to John Hodder Moggridge for 99 years. During 1794 Moggridge bought the freehold on the property.

The Church Street site was bought by Yerbury, Tugwell and Edmonds, clothiers, in 1807 and in January 1812 Yerbury sold his share which included the 'Red Lyon' (sic) property to Tugwell and Edmonds.[58] Little evidence of the Inn exists following this transaction.

From about 1820 Joseph Rawling ran his printing business there. In 1875 John James Rawling advertised his agency for the Wilts and Dorset Banking Co. By 1878, James Taylor, who then owned the house, sold out to the Wilts And Dorset Bank, and they converted it into a bank.[59]

Bertram Niblett, writing in 1981 states:

'A strongroom was specially constructed for security purposes (by the Wilts & Dorset Bank c.1878) and is still *in situ* in the drawing room of the house. The cellars of nos 2 & 3 Church Street were filled in at the same time as the strongroom was built, also for security reasons'.

By 1928 the house was sold to H.S. Bowyer, Builders.

2 Church Street. The blue plaque top left of the door commemorates the fact that this building was the Red Lion, then occupied by Rawlings the printer and latterly the Wilts.& Dorset Bank

Rising Sun 231 Winsley Road

An early mention of this house was in 1842 when John Blackmore was described as 'beer retailer only', it was not until 1861 that he was shown as Landlord of The Rising Sun. By 1908 Frank (Dodger) Mayell took over the premises, where he stayed as the Publican until his death in 1963 aged 102 years.

The Rising Sun was sold by Snailum Auctioneers of Trowbridge to Wilkins Brewery. Included in 1875 sale details were 'brewery plant, fixtures and fitting'.[60] Wilkins then sold the property on to Ushers Brewery in 1920.[61]

During the 1960 and '70s a group of rubber workers from the local Geo. Spencer Moulton Company who worked in the Extruding Department at the factory, used to meet regularly at the Rising Sun. Fellow workers used to call the pub the 'Extruders Arms'.

The present custodians at the pub are Dave and Liz Northeast who sell Real Ale and Good Cider, with Television showing sporting events, traditional pub games, including darts and cribbage teams.

The Rising Sun in Winsley Road, known locally as 'The Riser'

Riverside Inn

When English Heritage granted this building Grade Two listing in 1952, they referred to the house as late 17th with an 18th century wing extension. A further extension was added in the 1970s.

An early record of the house was in the late 1700s when Charles Spackman and his family were in residence. Charles was a Wool Dyer who died in 1844. He was followed by Joseph Rose and, by the 1870s, William Moore and family were living in the house, by then known as St Margaret's House. He was also a Wool Dyer employing 47 men in 1871. Moore was still there in 1903, remaining as wool dyer, with his nephew William Price as Dyer Manager. The Moore reign had ended by 1911. The Dyehouse for all the dyers who lived in St Margaret's House is the building now known as St Margaret's Hall. At this stage George Mead and his wife Elizabeth took up residence as stewards of The Tariff Reform Club.[62]

In addition to the Reform Club the house was used as a Constitutional Club and then as a Conservative Club.[63] The town library was also housed here for many years before moving in 1966 to a portakabin in St Margaret's Hall car park.

The Bradford Rowing Club took over the property around 1960 and erected a further extension, despite a serious fire. Unfortunately, due to financial reasons they could not continue in the building, It then became The Riverside Restaurant and then The Riverside Inn; it advertises itself as having original features, and all rooms have television and wi-fi access.

Rose and Crown Kingston Road

The Rose and Crown was situated at No. 2 Kingston Road. Until around 1885 the road was known as Mill Street.

An early mention of the inn was in the Land Tax assessments of 1773-4. By 1793, John Southwood was the innkeeper. Many innkeepers and owners of the property followed, some of whom were James Gerrish, Mary Long, Stephen Toghill, Thomas and Elizabeth Dancy, Henry Chilton, Henry Lewis, Alfred Blackmore, James Cross, Charles Earle, James Townsend, George Culverhouse, J. Forsyth, Henry Mead (who was also listed as Bookkeeper and Innkeeper), Herbert Earle, Thomas Andrews, Anthony Loch, Joseph Thomas Gore and Mrs Sarah Letita Rooke Cusse.[63]

The Rose and Crown supported the townsfolk by arranging a coach to Devizes Market every Thursday morning leaving the inn at 8 a.m. The service was still in operation in 1830.[63]

In August 1895 the Rose and Crown was bought by Brewers G. & T. Spencer's, in Whiteheads Lane, who established Herbert Earle as Publican. Earle only lasted one year, as did many others who followed.

During the Brewster Sessions at Bradford's Magistrates Court in 1907 it became obvious that the trade at the inn was decreasing, despite being so close to the Spencer Moulton rubber factory in Kingston Road.

An extract from the minutes of the meeting confirms this:

'evidence has shown that there were other licensed premises quite close, which were more adapted to modern requirements. The entrance to the Rose and Crown is through a dark court yard and the passages and lower rooms are badly lit. There is no stable accommodation. There have been frequent changes of tenants, and the sanitary arrangements are defective. On these grounds the Justices selected this licence for extinction.'

Spencer's the owners were informed and the Inn was closed in 1907 with Sarah Cusse as the last tenant.[65]

Royal Oak Shambles

This inn was located in the Shambles in the centre of town in the premises now occupied by Tillions shop, No. 6a the Shambles.

John Baber was the owner and Victualler at the Inn in 1731.[66]

By 1808 Ellenor Baber owned and occupied the Royal Oak, and as a result of her death in 1813, John Brimson Baber is recorded as the innkeeper until 1824, when ended a long reign of the Baber family.

View along The Shambles; note the hanging sign indicating The Royal Oak Inn, and the the licensee at the time, J.W. Smith

Overleaf: The Royal Oak's accounts drawn up showing declining sales prior to its closure in 1911

ROYAL OAK INN, Bradford-on-Avon.

ALE HOUSE, FULLY LICENSED.

Owners ... ... WILKINS BROS. & HUDSON, LTD.
Licensee ... ... ROBERT CLARKE.
Tied for Beers, Wines, Spirits and Aerated Waters.

Premises acquired by present owner ...	about 1887.
Income Tax {Schedule A	£21
{Schedule D	—
Inhabited House Duty	£21
Gross Estimated Rental	£21
Actual Rent Paid...	£13
Poor Rate Assessment {Gross ... ... }	Owners' Rates £6 18 0 per annum about.
{Rateable ... ... }	
Value of Trade fixtures—utensils	£29 0 5
Estimated Value of Premises without licence ...	£112
Estimated cost of conversion for purposes of }	£15
Letting or Sale without Licence ...}	
Rates and Taxes paid by Owners	{Rates £6 18 0 per annum (about)
	{Taxes
Ingoing	

TRADE DONE :—

				Cost Price per Barrel.	Charge to Customer per pint.
	1908.	1909.	1910.		
Beer, Ale and Double				XXXX 54/-	Beers and Double
Stout (barrels) ...	127⅝	99⅜	85⅜	XXX 45/-	2½d. or 3d.
				X 27/-	Ale 1½d.
				Double Stout 48/-	

				Cost Price per gallon.	Sale price per gallon.
Spirits, Irish Whisky,		gallons.			
Rum, Gin and Brandy	38	23½	18¾	Irish Whisky 19/8	26/8
				Rum 19/8	26/8
				Gin 14/8	18/8
				F. Brandy 22/10	42/8

Wines ... ... Nil.
Other Goods 1908. 1909. 1910.
  Mineral Waters 44 doz. 24 doz. 22 doz. ... profit 6d. per dozen.
  Tobacco ... 1lb. per week. ... Cost 4/11 ; selling at 5/4.

CLAIM FOR COMPENSATION :—

Average Trade ... 104 barrels of beer at 13/6 per barrel	...	...	70	4	0
26¾ gallons Wines and Spirits at 2/6 per gallon	...	...	3	6	10
30 doz. Minerals at 6d. per dozen	...	...	15		0
			74	5	10
Eleven years purchase					11
			817	4	2
Rent with Licence to yearly tenant ... 13 0 0					
At 20 years purchase... 20					
			260	0	0
Cost of Conversion of premises	...	...	15	0	0
Depreciation of Fixtures as per Valuer's Report	...	...	23	13	5
			1115	17	7
Less Value of premises unlicensed	...	...	112	0	0
TOTAL COMPENSATION CLAIMED ...		...	**1003**	**17**	**7**

Following the Babers numerous owners and tenants occupied the premises, some being Henry & Maria Fisher, John Rees Jones, William Hunt, John Long, David Marshman, John Edmonds, William & John (Jnr) Stokes, William Self, H. Crisp, John William Smith, John N. Smith, Albert Pike, Charles Matthews, John Saunders and Robert Clark.[67]

Around 1887, Wilkins Bros the brewers in Newtown, Bradford, bought the Royal Oak. Similar to many other inns in the town, the Royal Oak's trade began to dwindle and in 1907 the Licensing Justices reviewed the inn's licence and, after great deliberations, granted the licence. The inn managed to cling on to its licence until 1911 when the Justices again considered the licence. Following consultations with the owners, Messrs Wilkins Bros & Hudson Ltd., and licensee Robert Clark, the Justices resolved not to issue a licence. The inn was closed on 15th June 1911.

It is interesting to note that at that time, the prices paid by the licensee to the brewers for ale were :

> XXXX ale - 54/= (£2:70d) per barrel,
> XXX ale - 45/= (£2:25d) per barrel,
> X ale - 27/= (£1:35d) per barrel (no mention of XX ale!)
> Customers paid 3d. (1.25p) per pint for the XXXX ale.[62]

Wilkins Bros & Hudson held on to the ownership of the Royal Oak property, leasing it to various tenants. Eventually in 1920 they sold all their properties to Usher's, Brewers of Trowbridge. At the time of sale it was being used as an 'eating house and barbers shop.'[69]

Scribbling Horse Inn, later Lamb Inn

The 18th century clothiers house which once stood on the north side of the town bridge and lately the site of the Avon Rubber's building was, in the early 19th century the Scribbling Horse Inn. It was described in various records as being in Horse Street and sometimes as Bridge Foot.[70] It appears that Horse Street, at that time, stretched down from the sides of the Post Office and Swan Hotel buildings, towards the present roundabout, sweeping round to the end of the bridge.

In 1808 Daniel Collins was the landlord until George Notton occupied the Scribbling Horse in 1822. Licence applications before the magistrates in 1823/4 were also from Notton to license the Scribbling Horse, but in 1825 he had changed the name of the inn to the Lamb Inn, when he was granted a licence to cover the renamed inn which he occupied until 1836.[71] It was Notton who arranged for the carved stone lamb to be placed above the pillared entrance to the inn. The statue was to remain an imposing feature in the town for many years to come.

At this point Benjamin Matthews, who had previously been landlord of the New Inn, Bath Road, came to the Lamb Inn where he remained for some 12 years. Matthews combined innkeeping with saddle and harness making. It is interesting to note that the town's fire fighting equipment was housed near the Holy Trinity Church. The hose of the engine was made of leather, and was maintained by Benjamin Matthews.[75]

During this period the Lamb Inn was a base from which carriers operated. Stephen Mizen ran a local van route from the inn to Melksham and Devizes. Another left at 9am to Bath every weekday. In 1841 he set up a new service which was advertised in the local press as 'The new Bradford Omnibus leaving the Lamb at 7.30am daily, to reach the George Inn, Chippenham in time for the 10am train.'

From 1848 to 1889 a number of licensees occupied the inn, some being James Lewis, Thomas Holloway (Jnr), George F. Newman and Henry Edmund Tucker.[72]

In 1889, G. & T. Spencer, the Whiteheads Lane Brewers, bought the inn for £1,890, when they let the property to Matthew Hughes at £50 quarterly rent. From that date until 1911 the inn was trading well, with H. Willson, William Lewis, J. Macey, Henry and Eliza Mead, R. Broomfield and Frederick Lane being the tenants.[72] However during the Brewster Sessions of May 1911 the magistrates were confronted by a major problem regarding the issuing of a licence to the inn. The minutes of the session read:

> 'The Lamb is referred to the magistrates on the ground of being situated near to four other licensed houses, namely – 104 yds. from the Queens Head on the other side of the bridge, 57 yds. from the Royal Oak in the Shambles, and is immediately opposite the back entrance to the Swan, and 79 yds. from the Kings Arms Inn. It is affected by the river Avon when in flood, and the business done is very small, and the premises is in bad repair. There is no stabling.'

The magistrates considered the matter and resolved not to issue a new licence when the present licence expired in June 1912.[73] The inn closed its doors in June 1912 with Frederick Lane as its last landlord.

The building did not remain unoccupied for long. In September 1912 the directors and owners G. & T. Spencer's decided to let the old Lamb Inn 'as a common lodging house, at a rent of £16 per quarter'.

During May 1914, G. & T. Spencer's sold the building, together with their other properties in the town and elsewhere, to Usher's Brewery of Trowbridge. It is interesting to note that the official sale details stated that

'The late Lamb Inn – Formerly The Scribbling Horse Inn, Bradford, together with Brewhouse, Outhouse, Messuage and dwelling house'.

The reference to the former Scribbling Horse Inn confirms the change of name to the Lamb Inn in 1825, and referred to earlier.[1]

By 1916 the old Lamb building was in the hands of George Spencer, Moulton and Co Ltd., the local rubber manufacturers. In that year they demolished the property and by May a Bradford Town Council meeting approved plans for a new building on the site, which was completed by 1919, and still known today as the 'Lamb Building.'[74]

Talking to Bertram Niblett a few years before his death in 1988, he told me that following the demolition of the property, the stone lamb which had been in position since 1825 was taken to Mr Moulton's quarry near The Hall for safe keeping. Some while later it was discovered that vandals had smashed it to pieces.

One final point on this inn. The poet Edward Thomas, writing in his book *In Pursuit of Spring* in 1913 on the subject of his travels in the West Country, when reaching Bradford on Avon he wrote:

> 'I dismounted by the empty Lamb Inn with a statue of a black headed lamb over its porch, and sat on the bridge. The Avon ran swift, but calm and dull, down under the bridge and away westward.'

Perhaps the site appeared derelict and empty, as it did for some two decades until redevelopment finally got underway in 2009.

Seven Stars Newtown - see pages 29-35

Ship Inn later Carpenters Arms Inn, Church Street

In 1702 John Orpin was landlord and from 1716 to 1725 he also held The Swan. In 1731 William Orpin was landlord with part occupied by John Taplin in 1737. In 1739 Widow Taplin was named. In 1742 she married Edward Orpin, parish clerk. In 1769 the landlord was J. Taplin; in 1772-3 John Marshman.[75]

In 1808, a twin-gabled house in Church Street, situated between Church Hall and Church House was occupied by Mrs Linch as proprietress of the Ship Inn.[76] Between that date and 1851 the Ship Inn had a number of landlords, some of whom were William George Gibbs, James Kitson, Samuel Parsons, George Sheppard, John Cooper, Thomas Hedges, John Raynes Hayward and James Owen.[77] By 1852 the Inn had changed its name to the Carpenters Arms with Thomas Parker as landlord.[78]

In February 1884, Mrs Sarah Tucker kept the Carpenters Arms Inn and was involved in a divorce case which came before Judge, Sir James Hannen. Sarah petitioned for the dissolution of her marriage to her husband, David Tucker, on the grounds of cruelty and adultery. Their marriage had taken place on 2nd July 1866 at Bradford Church, she being a widow and he a widower. They then lived together at the Carpenters Arms as landlady and landlord.

The three-storeyed, twin-gabled Ship Inn, stood between the Masonic Hall to the left and the present Church House to the right. This plot is now a walled garden.

It was stated that in June 1867, in consequence of David Tucker's violence on her, she had summoned him before the magistrates and he was bound over to keep the peace. In 1882 he left her to reside at No. 48 Woolley Street, Bradford, where he carried on a business of Tiler and Plasterer. Sarah continued at the Carpenters Arms. Allegations were made and confirmed that David Tucker was seen on numerous occasions with a young woman named Alice Morris and seen going from the George Inn, Woolley Street to his house opposite, where they slept together. He was also accused of returning to the Carpenters Arms, threatening Sarah and repeatedly giving her black eyes. The Judge stated that there being no defence, the charges having been established, he pronounced a decree nisi with costs.[79]

Little is known why the inn changed its name to the Carpenters Arms, but a letter in the *Wiltshire Times and News* of the 28th July 1967 suggests a possible reason!

'It may not be commonly known that on the little piece of derelict land between Church House and Church Hall, in Church Street, there once stood a little Inn, it was called The Ship Inn, later it was known as The Carpenters Arms. Could it be that the name was changed when the present eyesore was erected opposite, thus shutting it off from the river?

No doubt the planning committee already have their eyes on this area. Here is an opportunity to make a real contribution to the town. The removal of these buildings together with the ugly remaining wall of the old Priory in Market Street would earn the gratitude of far more ratepayers than the extremely expensive swimming pool.

Signed 'A lover of Bradford'

Shortly after 1884 the inn was closed and by the mid-1920s the house was demolished.

The Swan Inn (Hotel) 1 Church Street

The Swan bears the date 1500 but was rebuilt in the 18th century. The inn was held by Sybella Clutton in 1629 and John Orpin in 1713; in 1730 the owner was Richard Yerbury and the occupier Francis Roche. By 1753 Richard Tayler was landlord. In 1791 The Swan was described as one of the two principal inns of the town. According to contemporary directories, from 1793 to '98 William Wall was victualler; William Hale is given in 1822 and again in 1842. In 1823 The Swan was the main centre from which carriers set out with their wagons and coaches which departed daily for Trowbridge, Bath and Bristol.[80] By 1865 John Cosburn Neale is given as landlord of the Swan Hotel, Commercial Inn and posting house, and Inland Revenue Office.

There were few residents who received a daily newspaper, or even a weekly one, in those days, their being too expensive for the many. The traders of the town usually met in what was called The Tradesmen Room, at the inn, to hear and see the news, talk over the trade, helping each other to a pinch of snuff, a whiff of tobacco, or sip of the celebrated Bradford XXX beer. At the time all magisterial and other town business, took place in the Long Room at the Inn.[81]

The Old Town Market Hall at the end of the Shambles, nearest the Kings Arms, had disappeared by the 1820s so the Courts Leet had also began to use the Swan for

One too many?

⋆⊱ SWAN ⊰⋆
Family and Commercial Hotel
AND POSTING HOUSE,
BRADFORD - ON - AVON.

H. A. NORRIS

Tenders his sincere thanks to his patrons for the support he has received as Proprietor of the above old established Hotel, and assures them that every attention shall continue to be paid to the comfort and convenience of those who may honor him with their future favors.

WINES, SPIRITS AND CIGARS.
Home-brewed Beer and Ale in Casks of all sizes.
OAKHILL PORTER.

Superior Accommodation for Commercial Gentlemen combined with moderate charges.

FLYS, PHÆTONS & WAGONETTES,
ON HIRE ON THE SHORTEST NOTICE.
HORSES, CARRIAGES & BREAKS
Of every description for Pleasure Parties, Weddings, &c.

⋆⋆⋆ BILLIARDS. ⋆⋆⋆

Advertisement for The Swan in Farrington's 1888 Town Directory

its meetings. In addition the Excise Office occupied a room here. The new Town hall was built in 1855, so all public gatherings before this date were at the Swan.[82]

Advertisement from Dotesio's 1902 Directory attempting to attract motorists and cyclists with ping-pong as well as the more traditional billiards.

Three Horse Shoes Inn 56 Frome Road

An early record of 1793/8 indicates that Thomas Harding was innkeeper at this coaching inn and William Hale Jnr was *in situ* in 1822/4. There was formerly a large garden at the rear of the premises, but much of it was taken over by the Railway Company around 1850, for the yard in front of the station. The Steed family was in residence 1898-1913. During a sale of their properties in 1920 the Wilkins Brewery, sold the inn to Ushers Brewery. The sale inventory included, inn with cottage, used as a cobblers shop, adjoining on the north side.[83]

Many other innkeepers followed, with William Norris taking over about 1931. He was the landlord who, at closing time would walk around the pub clanging, very loudly his large bunch of keys. He called out 'Time Gentlemen Please' several times and customers were expected to drink up and go immediately. In 1939 an out building was listed, as an air raid shelter for the local area, by 1940 it was declared unsafe for purpose.

Frederick and Phylis Billett managed the pub through the 1950s. Sadly, in 1959 Fred was found dead in the cellar, having committed suicide. This was a great surprise to all. His wife Phyllis carried on as manageress for several years with the help of their son Tony. The premises were refurbished following the Billetts' departure. It was transformed with a pleasant restaurant area and was very popular for a time.

The Three Horse Shoes Inn which grew in importance with the coming of the railway

Landaus, Brakes, Wagonettes and Traps on Hire.

Three Horse Shoes Inn,

·.· BRADFORD=ON=AVON. ·.·

The Old Established Posting House,

One Minute's Walk from the Railway Station.

SINGLE OR PAIR-HORSE CARRIAGES,

For Weddings or Pic-nic Parties.

L. STEEDS,

Proprietress.

Recently the Official Pub Guide wrote, 'This pub does not serve food. It is a no frills traditional pub, which has a friendly welcoming atmosphere attracting leather jackets to suits, muddy boots to shiny shoes and comb overs to mohicans. Selections of snacks are available, including crisps and nuts, on offer all day, every day.'

White Hart, Market Street/Silver Street

The White Hart stood at the junction of Market Street and Silver Street, in recent years known as Knee's Corner and now a paved seating area.

In 1731 Benjamin Cooper was the innkeeper and in February of that year he appeared in a Quarter Session case at Devizes which caused quite a furore in the town, more on that later.[84]

Benjamin Spender was the innkeeper in 1808 and following his death aged 61 years in 1838, Sarah Spender took over the reins at the inn until her demise in 1851 aged 65 years. Thomas Spender continued the family tradition with his sisters until 1866, when he decided to retire, and the 'White Hart Inn and Brewery' were sold by auction on 19th December 1865 at the Swan Hotel, Bradford-on-Avon. The sale details included:

[Lot 1] 'Bar, Bar Parlour, large Tap Room, Sitting Room, Wash House, and three capital Cellars on the ground floor ; also a front Sitting Room, and five bedrooms.There is also a good Brewery, Malt and Hop Room and Store Room, with a capital well of water and force pump on the premises.'

It is interesting to note that at the same auction:

[Lot 2] 'Dwelling house situated in the Old Market Place, adjoining the Inn, containing a Front Shop, Kitchen, four bedrooms, and attic over. There is a pump and well of water in the back kitchen. These premises have a frontage of 112 ft; there is sufficient space by converting the premises adjoining the Inn, to carry on an extensive Brewing business.'

Following the Spender family, Edward Streeter came to the premises in 1866. Other occupiers were Mr Daniels, Daniel S. Smith and Henry Arthur Reed.

The White Hart was sold in 1878 to Rev. Mr Thring of Chantry House who reconstructed the building five feet back to allow for road widening. It opened as Bradford Temperance Tavern in August 1879. The architect was C. Adye.

H.J. Knee, the Trowbridge Furnishers bought the building in 1908, and rather disappointingly it was demolished in 1967, thus allowing better visibility for motorists.

Excessive drinking in the town is not just a present day problem, which is well illustrated by the following article involving the White Hart's innkeeper, Benjamin Cooper:

On Monday 22nd February 1731, Bradford magistrate Thomas Methuen was presiding at court. Churchwarden Richard Burcombe brought John Rogers before Methuen on a charge of tippling (drinking) at the White Hart during the hours of divine service on the previous day. Innkeeper Benjamin Cooper of the White Hart was also charged for permitting it to occur. Both were found guilty and Rogers was put into the stocks on the following Friday.

The stocks were positioned at the market house (at the end of the Shambles, adjoining Tillions), only a short distance from the White Hart. The closeness of the Tavern played a major part in the events which followed, and resulted in Rogers, Cooper and others to appear at Devizes Quarter Sessions on 27th. April 1731, on the charge of riotous assembly.

The White Hart at the former Knees Corner, where Market and Silver Streets meet. The Royal Oak can be seen along Silver Street.

In addition to Rogers and Cooper, William and Joseph Dicke and Gabriel Cox amongst others were grouped at the stocks, and were accused of holding a riotous party at the scene. A female servant from the White Hart brought a plate of meat from her master's kitchen and placed it near the incarcerated Rogers together with a silver tankard of ale for him to drink. Further ale was brought from the inn for all to consume.

Witnesses were called, when they expressed that it was obvious that the assembly at the stocks disagreed with the action taken against Rogers by Burcombe and Methuen. James Miles of Bradford, a baker, stated that as he was riding through the market area, William Dicke hailed him calling, "Miles, look here James, see what one of the pillars of the church has done out of malice" referring to Burcombe. Further witnesses spoke of shouting, with words against Burcombe. During this raucous period, Edward Robert, a boy, was beating a drum in the market area and William Dicke summoned him to beat his drum near the stocks, which he did.

At this point, the Parish Constable intervened, as the situation was getting out of control. He ordered the boy to stop beating his drum, which prompted Dicke to shout more abuse at the Constable. Fearing a riot situation, Rogers was released from the stocks, but the boy continued to beat his drum, and accompanied Rogers with his friends back to the White Hart.

More witnesses gave evidence against the mob. One said that William Dicke called to passers by 'this is the work of Burcombe who receives the Sacrament and then informs against a fellow out of malice.'

White Lion, Huntingdon Place
The only reference to this Inn is in Bertram Niblett's *Memories Of Bradford-on-Avon*. He wrote 'In Huntingdon Place was the White Lion'. It is possible that Nos 5 & 6 Huntingdon Place, once one house, was the building referred to.

White Lion, Newtown
An early reference to the Inn was in 1793 when Benjamin Spender, who had bought the premises from Paul Methuen Esq. was in residence. The house, now 39 Newtown, was left to his son, also Benjamin Spender, in his father's will of 1796.[86]

By 1808 Benjamin, Jun. was at the White Hart in the centre of town.

Adam Clark took over from him and he was followed as landlord or owner by William and Joanna Mundy, Robert Price, Mary Spender, John Cottle, James and Hazell Chapman and William Norris also referred to as Boatman as well as Innkeeper.[87]

The last reference to the Inn was in 1863 when the town's licensing authorities received an application from Richard Bendy, Victualler, of he White Lion, Newtown, to transfer the licence to James Snook, Innkeeper, then residing at Road (Rode) in the parish of North Bradley.[88]

As mentioned earlier in the Seven Stars item, sometime during the lifetime of the Inn, the Hudson family owned the property, together with a small brewery at the White Lion. The Hudson family lived at the Lynchetts, Woolley Street.[89]

In later years the building was occupied by William Penny, Grocer and Baker. Many present-day Bradfordians will remember this family business. By 1958 Mr F.A. Brooks, also a baker was in residence.[2] The house is now a private home. It is possible, with some difficulty, to make out the lettering in a band above the first floor windows which read 'HOME BREWED ALES & BEERS'.

Town Bridge Lock-up

It is possible that when townsfolk had visited a number of the town's inns in the mid-19th century and were a little inebriated and belligerent, the magistrates or town constable would order the person to be placed in the lock-up on the bridge.

Perhaps this happened in 1821 when Triphma White was apprehended and brought before the magistrate and spent the night in the cell. This action earned the constable, Robert Price 5 shillings (25p) for his trouble.[90]

By 1825 William Taylor was the town constable. At 8 o'clock one evening in October 1825, William Palmer was arrested by Taylor for insulting behaviour against Daniel Fleming and his sister in William Taylor's shop. Palmer appeared to 'have drunk some beer' but was not much intoxicated, at least he was not in a state of regular 'Bradford drunkenness'. Taylor tied and fastened Palmer's arms with a rope, led him through the town of Bradford and afterwards confined him to the 'blind house' on the bridge.

Palmer complained to Taylor that the cell in the blind house was in the most shocking state. The straw was putrefying, occasioning the most disagreeable smell, that several persons had been confined there without the dung being cleansed, that there was no seat in the room. On the Sunday the constable had it cleared out, admitting it was in a shocking state.

Palmer was liberated on the Monday prior to his appearance before the court that morning. He was discharged on the understanding that he would leave the town and county and never be brought before the court again.[1]

It was after this date that a dividing wall and two iron bedsteads were erected on the walls and rings for the attachment of shackles were also installed. A latrine hole down to the river below was also made at this time.

In a book entitled *Life on the Hill: Colerne Remembered* a villager recalled 'my father-in-law was the village policeman. He was at Trowbridge, Corsham and Bradford-on-Avon and all the way around. He said he used to lock them up at Bradford, there was a little 'house' over the bridge. If a drunkard couldn't get home he used to lock him in there and go and unlock him in the morning.'

The town bridge lock-up is surmounted by a gudgeon, a fish found in the River Avon and a symbol of Bradford. Hence the local saying 'Under the Bridge and Over the Water', a euphemism used to refer to someone being held in the lock-up.

Notes and References

The Story of Ale

1 Jefferies, Richard: *The Hills and the Vale*, 1875
2 Cunningham, B. Howard (ed.): Extracts from the records of the County of Wiltshire, 1932
3 Extracts from the Records of the County of Wiltshire. Quarter Sessions, 1682
4 Burke, Thomas: *The English Inn*, 1930
5 Jefferies, Richard: *The Open Air*, 1889

The Seven Stars, Newtown:
Public House and Brewery

1 Wiltshire Buildings Record
2 W.R.O. Cat. G13
3 W.R.O. Cat. 1454
4 Niblett, Bertram S.: *Memories of Bradford-on-Avon*. Wiltshire Library & Museum Service, 1981
5 W.R.O. Cat. 1075/582
6 W.R.O. Cat. G13/760
7 *Devizes & Wiltshire Gazette*
8 *Wiltshire News*
9 Jack Stafford
10 W.R.O.Cat 1075/103

Spencer's Brewery

1 Pigots Directory, 1822
2 Powell, W.R.: *History of Bradford on Avon*. Wiltshire Library and Museum Service, 1990
3 A1/355/2: Electoral Register
4 Robson's Directory, 1838
5 Fassnidge, Harold: *Bradford on Avon Past & Present*. Ex Libris Press, 1988, 1997 and 2007
6 Langdon, Gee: *Year of the Map: Portrait of a Wiltshire Town in 1841*. Compton Russell, 1976
7 Tithe Schedule, 1842
8 W.R.O. Cat 1075/595/1
9 W.R.O. Cat 1075/595/2
10 Rawlings Directories, 1890-1895
11 W.R.O. Cat A1/615
12 Rogers, Ken: *Wiltshire & Somerset Woollen Mills*. Pasold Research Fund Ltd

The King's Arms and Brewery

1 *Heritage Journal*, 1975
2 Ken Rogers
3 Cat No A1/615: Licensing of Public Houses
4 Cat No G13/990/28
5 Bradford Directories, 1907
6 *Kelly's Directory*, 1911
7 *Wiltshire Times*, 1916
8 Niblett, Bertram S.: *Memories of Bradford-on-Avon*. Wiltshire Library & Museum Service, 1981
9 Alec Wiltshire
10 Jack Stafford

Other Malthouses and Breweries

1 WRO Cat 1742 Methuen Archives
2 WRO Cat G13/990/18
3 WRO Cat 687/4
4 WRO Cat 687/27
5 WRO Cat 973/11 Deeds
6 Roger Mawby
7 Slocombe, Pam: *Wiltshire Farmhouses and Cottages, 1500-1800*. Devizes Book Press, 1992
8 1841 Tithe Map
9 Fassnidge, Harold: *Bradford on Avon Past & Present*. Ex Libris Press, 1988, 1997 and 2007
10 Auctioneers A/C's W.R.O. 2623/59

Bradford on Avon's Pubs

1 Cat 1075/001/35 W.R.O.
2 Cat 1075/595/ 2 W.R.O.
3 *Wiltshire Times*, July 2010
4 cat A1/363/3 W.R.O.
4 W.R.O. Cat 1075
5 Western Daily Press, 1997
6 Wiltshire News, 1928
7 G13/990/34 W.R.O.
8 Bradford Museum
9 Langdon, Gee: *Year of the Map: Portrait of a Wiltshire Town in 1841*. Compton Russell, 1976
10 CAT D632/2/2 W.R.O.
11 Langdon, Gee: *Year of the Map: Portrait of a Wiltshire Town in 1841*. Compton Russell, 1976
12 Recognizances

13 Fassnidge, Harold: *Bradford on Avon Past & Present*. Ex Libris Press, 1988, 1997 and 2007

14 Langdon, Gee: *Year of the Map: Portrait of a Wiltshire Town in 1841*. Compton Russell, 1976

15 Census

16 *Kelly's Directory*

17 Bradford Museum

18 Street Directory

19 CAT 1075/595/W.R.O.

20 Powell, W.R.: *History of Bradford on Avon*. Wiltshire Library and Museum Service, 1990

21 Langdon, Gee: *Year of the Map: Portrait of a Wiltshire Town in 1841*. Compton Russell, 1976

22 Niblett, Bertram S.: *Memories of Bradford-on-Avon*. Wiltshire Library & Museum Service, 1982

23 Street Directory

24 Rate Assessments

25 W.R.O. Cat. 1075

26 W.R.O. Cat. 800

27 Shehan, John C.: *History of the Bradford on Avon Club*

28 Niblett, Bertram S.: *Memories of Bradford-on-Avon*. Wiltshire Library & Museum Service, 1982

29 Directories

30 Roger Mawby

31 W.R.O. Cat 212

32 W.R.O. Cat 1075

33 S.A.J. Boxwell

34 *Victoria County History: Wiltshire*

35 W.R.O. Cat 77

36 W.R.O. Cat 17422

37 Wiltshire Buildings Record

38 D.M. Anderson

39 W.R.O. Cat A1

40 Directories

41 Anderson, D.M.: *Heritage,* 1975

42 Powell, W.R.: *History of Bradford on Avon*. Wiltshire Library and Museum Service, 1990

43 CAT 1075/595/2 W.R.O.

44 Street Directories

45 CAT 1075/595/2 W.R.O.

46 Bradford Museum

47 Street Directories

48 D.O.E. Listed Buildings

49 Wiltshire Buildings Record

50 Directories

51 Langdon, Gee: *Year of the Map: Portrait of a Wiltshire Town in 1841*. Compton Russell, 1976

52 *Trowbridge Chronicle*

53 W.R.O. Cat A1

54 W.R.O. Cat G13

55 Alec Wiltshire

56 *Wiltshire News*

57 Tithe Map

58 Deeds, privately owned

59 Fassnidge, Harold: *Bradford on Avon Past & Present*. Ex Libris Press, 1988, 1997 and 2007

60 CAT 1039/30 W.R.O.

61 CAT 1075/582/1 W.R.O.

62 Census Returns

63 Niblett, Bertram S.: *Memories of Bradford-on-Avon*. Wiltshire Library & Museum Service, 1982

64 Directories

65 W.R.O. Cat. A1

66 Quarter Sessions

67 Street Directories

68 W.R.O. Cat. A1

69 W.R.O. Cat. 1075

70 W.R.O. Cat 1075

71 W.R.O. Cat A1/363

72 Street Directories

73 W.R.O. Cat A1/615

74 W.R.O. Cat G13

75 Wiltshire Buildings Record

76 Rate Assessment

77 Recognizances

78 Directories

79 *Wiltshire Times*

80 Anderson, D.M.: Heritage

81 50 Years Progress, 1837-1887

82 Langdon, Gee: *Year of the Map: Portrait of a Wiltshire Town in 1841*. Compton Russell, 1976

83 CAT 1075/582/1 W.R.O.

84 Quarter Sessions

85 Directories

86 W.R.O. Wills

87 Directories

88 W.R.O. Licence Applications

89 Niblett, Bertram S.: *Memories of Bradford-on-Avon*. Wiltshire Library & Museum Service, 1981

Town Bridge Lock-up

90 *Devizes and Wiltshire Gazette*, 1825

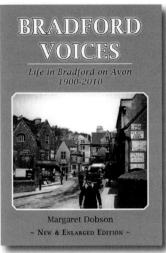